D0973134

# How to Make
# MISSION STYLE
# LAMPS AND SHADES

# How to Make
# MISSION STYLE
# LAMPS AND SHADES

Popular Mechanics Company

DOVER PUBLICATIONS, INC.
NEW YORK

Published in Canada by General Publishing Company, Ltd.,
30 Lesmill Road, Don Mills, Toronto, Ontario.
Published in the United Kingdom by Constable & Company,
Ltd.

This Dover edition, first published in 1982, is an unabridged
republication of the work written by John D. Adams and first
published in 1911 by the Popular Mechanics Company, Chicago,
under the title *Lamps and Shades in Metal and Art Glass:
Eighteen Complete Designs and Shades in Drawings and Full
Directions for Their Making*. The Note on the Dover Edition,
which incorporates the preface of the original edition, has been
added to the Dover edition. Except for minor changes in typog-
raphy for the sake of clarity, the text and illustrations of the
original edition are unaltered in every respect.

Manufactured in the United States of America

Dover Publications, Inc.
180 Varick Street
New York, N.Y. 10014

Library of Congress Cataloging in Publication Data

Adams, John Duncan, 1879–
  How to make mission style lamps and shades.

  Reprint. Originally published: Lamps and shades in metal and
art glass. Chicago: Popular Mechanics Co., 1911. (Popular mechanics handbooks)
  1. Lamps. 2. Lampshades. 3. Furniture, Mission.
I. Title. II. Series.
TT897.2.A3 1982          749'.63          81-17308
ISBN 0-486-24244-7                        AACR2

## A NOTE ON THE DOVER EDITION

This volume, written by an expert in the field, presents in clear, straightforward language all the requisite information for making the projects illustrated herein. None of the materials required are extravagantly priced or otherwise difficult to obtain. Thus this Dover republication makes available—in a high-quality paperback edition and at a very low price—the fundamental instructions for making lamps and shades in the distinctive Mission style.

*How to Make Mission Style Lamps and Shades* was originally published in 1911 by the Popular Mechanics Company (see copyright page for details) as a part of a series of crafts books. The reader will note occasional references to other books in the series, none currently available, with the exception of *Mission Furniture: How to Make It* (New York: Dover Publications, 1980), which combines three Popular Mechanics volumes into one. Dover Publications trusts that readers will keep in mind the date of the original edition, and not expect to purchase materials at the prices quoted in the text. Passing references to the "gentle sex" also appear in the text; it is the publisher's hope that such references will be met with the smile that expressions of past fashion deserve.

# INTRODUCTION

IN one of the Popular Mechanics Handbooks ("Arts-Crafts Lamps—How to Make Them") the writer has described the method of constructing substantial and attractive Arts-and-Crafts lamps from such simple materials as colored paper and cardboard. In this book are presented a series of articles on home-made lamps in the construction of which metal and glass are utilized.

The subject of lamps appeals to the amateur craftsman for four reasons:—the importance of a good and conveniently arranged light; the pleasing decorative effects that are possible; the variety and number of lamps that may be used to advantage in the home; and the small cost of equipment and necessary materials.

In the handbook referred to above are given designs for a wide diversity of lamps. In the chapters which follow the intent is to thoroughly acquaint the reader with the several methods of construction that come within the scope of the amateur's modest workbench, so that, having learned these and the subsequent possibilities, no difficulty will be found in executing in glass and metal, instead of paper and cardboard, the designs of my first book as well as those elaborated in these pages.

"It is easy when you know how," is a saying that is as true as it is trite when applied to our subject; and the writer has never yet in his experience with the manual arts seen disappointment reward the amateur's efforts in this line of work. Of course, one must have that enthusiasm and interest that begets patience; for with haste there is nothing but failure. One must be willing to take a block of wood and trim it up squarely, smooth the end grain, bevel off the upper corners, all with mathematical accuracy, or the base of the lamp will not have the true finished effect. This means patience and the steel square —but that is all.

Besides a little simple carpentry, the reader should be able to soft-solder, use a small breast drill, and properly set small rivets. The use of the lathe or other machine tool, forge or furnace, is not required. A good bench, a vise, a small assortment of drills, a hacksaw, a fretsaw, a hammer, a soldering-iron, are about all that are required.

There are four distinct methods of making lamp shades that are available for home construction:

1. *Built-up Shades*—Those having their frames built up from strips and angles of brass and copper.

2. *Soldered Shades*—Those in which each section or piece of glass is bound around its edges with thin metal, so that the whole may be soldered together.

3. *Etched Shades*—Those in which the openings in the metal are eaten or etched out by acid.

4. *Sawn Shades*—Those in which the metal design is sawn out with a small fretsaw.

Such is the general method of subdividing our subject, and no attempt will be made at any classification based on the type of lamp. Our object is primarily to set forth the different constructive methods available.

In regard to the construction of the bases and standards, the method to be presented is particularly adapted to home construction. Metal castings, stampings, spun metal and forgings are all avoided. Wood, used in connection with such simple pieces of brass and copper as may be easily shaped, forms the basis of construction. Let the wood be accurately and smoothly finished, stained with some reference to the general color scheme of the room in which it is to be used, polished so as to develop the graining, and finally trimmed with the necessary pieces of brass or copper; and we have a combination of materials of pleasing contrast and susceptible of very artistic treatment.

As there are so many beautiful kinds of glass to be had, no attempt will be made to refer to each variety by its trade name, so that the general expression "art glass" will be used throughout. Frosted, mottled, iridescent, watered, opalescent and butterfly effects may all be seen in any large fixture store. If your local dealer can not supply you, or direct you to the proper source, send a paper pattern to some dealer in manual training supplies.

*NOTE: Throughout this book all measurements are stated in inches, and for that reason the conventional sign has been omitted.*

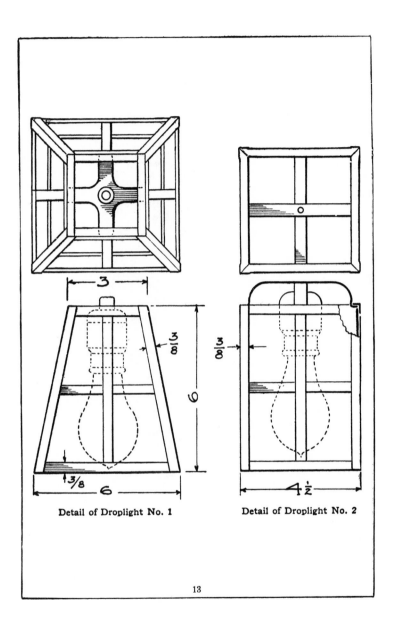

Detail of Droplight No. 1

Detail of Droplight No. 2

Droplight No. 1

(For detail working drawing see preceding page)

# PART ONE — BUILT-UP SHADES

## CHAPTER I

### DROPLIGHTS

THE simplest form of built-up shade is that used for droplights and may be made with either parallel or slanting sides, as shown in the illustration. Let us consider the parallel form.

First procure a small supply of sheet brass not over one-fiftieth of an inch in thickness, and even less for the narrow crossbars. Mark out on this the strips that will be necessary to form the various angles—twelve in all— and then accurately cut them. If a tinshop is in the vicinity, take the brass there and cut it on the foot trimmer, as there will then be no curling or twisting of the strips. Get clearly in the mind the relative positions of the one vertical and two horizontal members at each corner where they make a triple connection; and then trim off the strips to the exact lengths. Two or three dressed strips of hardwood should now be obtained, so that the strips may be properly held in the vise and without marring them. Draw a line accurately down the center of each strip to be bent, and then clamp them between the hardwood strips as shown in Fig. 1. The bending should then be done with the edge of a third strip of wood, the lower edge of which must be kept well down toward the vise so as to make a sharp bend. A uniform strip of angular section can be produced only when the bending has been done uniformly along the entire length

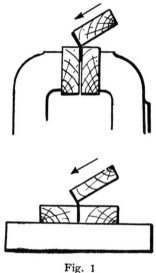

Fig. 1

Substitute for a Vise

at the same time. If it is necessary to use a hammer in finishing apply it to the block, hitting rather lightly, and never twice in the same place in succession. Should a vise not be available, the next best plan is to fasten two strips of hardwood to a piece of board, leaving a very small slit between them, into which the strip of metal may be placed for bending, as shown in the lower part of Fig. 1.

Droplight No. 2

In connecting up, the four angle strips of any one side are first joined, after which the vertical and horizontal crossbars are inserted. The four members of the side directly opposite are then to be connected in the same manner, after which the two complete sides so formed are connected by the four remaining angle strips—one at the top and bottom of each of the other two sides. It will usually be found advisable to use small rivets at the top connections, which hold the pieces together in a manner that permits their being adjusted squarely as the bottom pieces are placed and soldered.

To hang the shade, either one of two methods may be adopted. The simplest way is to provide two strips of rather heavier brass and bend their ends so that they will arch across the top as shown. At the place of crossing a hole is bored for the cord to pass through, and the four ends are riveted or soldered to the top angle strips. The shade will then hang directly on the top of the socket.

In the second and more substantial method, a crosspiece is provided with a hole large enough to allow the nipple in the top of the socket to pass, as shown in Fig. 2. These nipples, when of metal, are usually doubleended, in which case the upper portion must be sawn off with the hacksaw.

In the tapering form of drop shade the general method of construction is identical, except that there are practically no right angles. One should first lay out the shade full size and with sufficient accuracy to enable all angles being measured direct from the plat. The upper corner angles are quite a little larger than 90°, and the lower ones naturally as much less. Before proceeding with the bending, place the two strips of hardwood in the vise and plane off the upper edges at the proper angle. The upper angle strips may then be bent up the

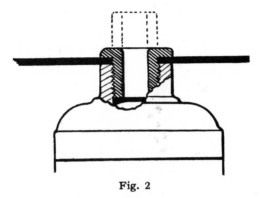

Fig. 2

Method of Hanging a Shade

slope, and the lower ones down. In this way we get one angle as much more as the other is less than 90°.

When the entire frame has been assembled, brighten up the outer surfaces with some old emery cloth, after which apply a coat of lacquer. Even ordinary frosted glass makes an excellent appearance with a finish of this character.

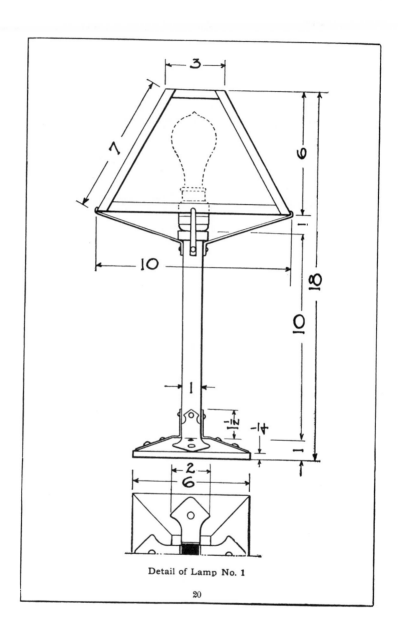

Detail of Lamp No. 1

Reading Lamp No. 1

# CHAPTER II

## READING LAMP NUMBER ONE

LET us now carry out on a somewhat more extensive scale the method described in the previous chapter for making a brass lamp-shade frame, and as a reward we shall have the attractive reading lamp that forms the subject of the accompanying illustration. It should be remembered, however, that without color our illustration does poor justice to this lamp, much less giving any adequate idea of the appearance when illuminated. The glass is of a milky white streaked with blue, and when lit up is very suggestive of sky and water. The scenic effect is made from thin brass, hammer-marked and somewhat oxidized, which appears a dead black at night.

The first step will be to make a plat of one side of the shade, noting that the slant distance is 7 in. and not 6 in. From a consideration of this determine the amount of material necessary, and get clearly in mind the method of making the triple connection at each corner. If any doubt exists on these points, it would be well to cut and bend into angles some strips of light cardboard or thin tin, so that a preliminary frame may be constructed. The various pieces of the temporary structure may then be taken apart and flattened out to serve as patterns in working up the brass or copper.

Having bent the twelve angle strips between wood, as described in the preceding chapter, the four members of one side should be soldered or sweated together. The opposite side is next formed, and then connected to the first by means of the four remaining angle strips. During the setting up, keep the plat constantly at hand so that all angles will be correct and uniform.

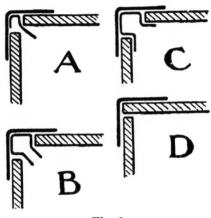

Fig. 3

**Securing the Glass in Place**

Some simple scenes should be decided upon and then drawn out on paper full size. Procure the necessary amount of thin (say, one-sixty-fourth) brass or copper, and transfer the designs thereto by means of carbon transfer paper. Cut out with the tin-snips, and then beat up the design with the ball end of the hammer over a block of hardwood. Foliage, tree trunks, etc., should be accentuated. The metal should then be thoroughly cleaned with soap and water, after which it may be dark-

ened by a solution of potassium sulphide and water.
Copper may be colored by simply heating to the proper
degree. A little fine emery or pumice is then used to rub
up the highlights, after which the pieces are attached to
the frame by tacking them with solder to the inside of

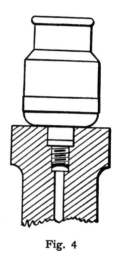

Fig. 4

Attaching Socket to Standard

the corner angle strips. A paper pattern is now to be
made so that the glass may be properly ordered. To secure this in place we may solder into the corner angles
some small pieces of brass, as at A in Fig. 3, which are
bent over when the glass is placed. Where a little more
space is available, adopt the method shown at B, bending
the two ends over onto the glass, as at C. If the glass is
heavy and accurately fitted, as at D, only two of the four

pieces need be secured, and these only at the top and bottom.

The base of the lamp is composed of a single block of wood, which is completely beveled off on top, with the exception of a space 2 in. square, in the center of which a ¾-in. square hole is mortised to receive the end of the standard, which is now to be gotten out and tenoned to match. The upper end of the standard is built out so as to form a cap, and is then drilled out for the socket to fit in, as shown in Fig. 4. See that the nipple is securely screwed into the socket and fits tightly into the wood. When ready to screw it down, apply a little glue to harden the fibers and fill all interstices. Drill a ⅜-in. hole lengthwise clear through the standard, and then cut a groove in the under side of the base—all for holding the electric cord. Attach the base and standard together with glue on the mortise-and-tenon joint. When dry, apply the necessary stain and filler, and polish with wax when dry. Prepare the four brass or copper brackets and attach them with round-head screws. The four thin bracket arms that support the shade are now to be made and attached, after which the placing of the shade in position completes the lamp.

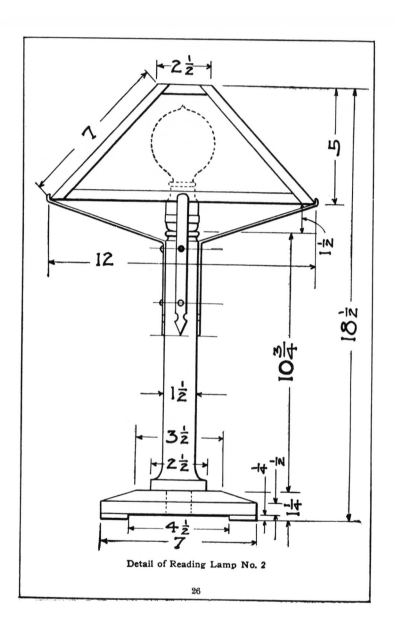

Detail of Reading Lamp No. 2

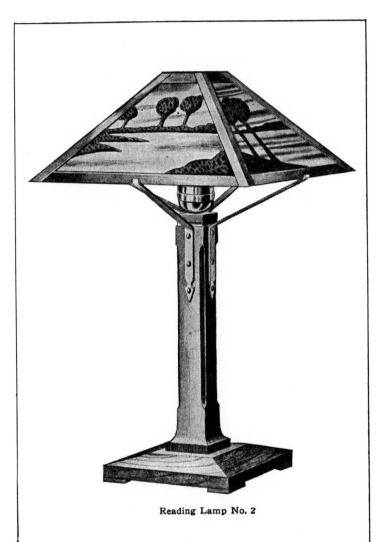

Reading Lamp No. 2

# CHAPTER III

IN offering a second lamp with a scenic shade it is not our intention to go over the ground of the preceding chapter, but rather to point out some of the modifications possible with this interesting type of lamp.

In the first place it will be noted that the shade has a greater spread and less of a slope than reading lamp No. 1, thus making it better adapted to a 32-candlepower or even a strong tungsten light. The socket should be operated by a drop pull.

If desired, the entire framework of the shade may be made of copper and thoroughly hammered, in which case it will be found best to do the hammering before forming the strips into angles. Should the strips become hardened during the process, soften them by heating over the gas flame. On account of the sharp angle of the shade the reader will do well to visit the local tinshop and secure some thin, flat strips of tin, from which he can make and fit a preliminary frame, thus avoiding all danger of spoiling the copper. In this manner all angles involved may be made plain and the entire task greatly simplified. The metal is now to be colored by oxidizing it with some solution such as potassium sulphide and water, after which rub up the highlights and apply a coat of lacquer to make the effect permanent.

A new feature in the metal work of this lamp is the

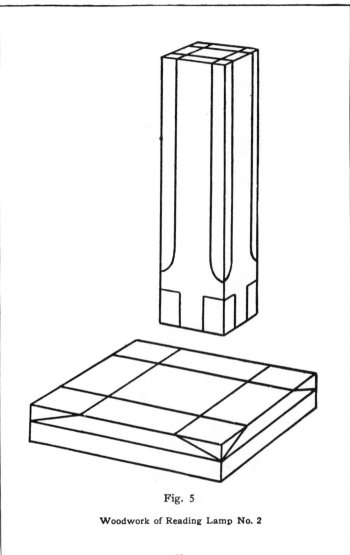

Fig. 5

Woodwork of Reading Lamp No. 2

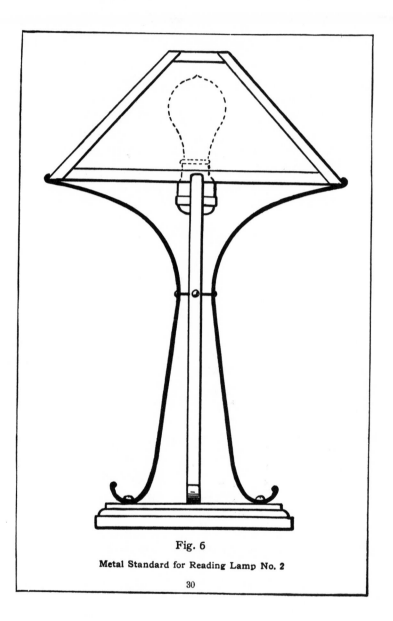

Fig. 6

**Metal Standard for Reading Lamp No. 2**

lengthened brackets that support the shade. These should be made of stock measuring ⅛ in. by ½ in., and may be trimmed up on their lower ends in any attractive form. Attach them with round-head brass screws. And by the way, let not the reader imagine that there is anything inherently inartistic in screwheads, or that there is any great reason why we should go out of our way to conceal them. Carefully finished metal on well finished wood has the peculiar attractiveness of a scientific instrument. But the effect is entirely lost if the screwheads are rough or burred. Place each screw in the breast drill, which is then clamped in the vise so that one hand will be free to polish the head with old emery cloth.

The woodwork of this lamp will require some little care on the part of those whose experience in carpentry is just beginning. After trimming up squarely and to the exact size, the base block should first be marked as in Fig. 5. Saw off first the two slices that run across the grain. Plane down to line before cutting off the other two slices. Use sandpaper only when placed on a small block, so that all surfaces will be flat, and all angles and corners sharp. The four small feet are now to be glued and tacked on with small brads, allowing them to project a trifle beyond the base, so that when the glue has set they can be trimmed off exactly flush. Mortise a 1-in. hole in the center.

The standard will also present some opportunity for accurate work, on account of the widened base and the attached tenon that fits into the base. Trim up the piece of timber accurately, and then mark it off with guide

lines, as in Fig. 5. First saw out two sides directly opposite and finish these down to line before cutting into a
third side. Of course, this job might be delegated to the
neighboring carpenter, but in that case our lamp would
not be strictly home-made. Work slowly and without

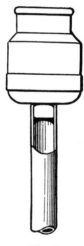

Fig. 7

Attaching Socket to Metal Standard

hurry, keeping the try-square at hand, and all will go well.
The central hole for the cord should be about the size of
a lead-pencil, and on account of its length will have to be
drilled from both ends. Set up the mortise-and-tenon
joint with glue and clamp firmly until dry.

The stain must be evenly applied. When dry, put on
a coat of filler, rubbing off all the surplus from the sur-

face. When this has dried well, the piece is to be lightly sandpapered, and then rubbed up with wax.

Attach the socket to the standard as shown in Fig. 4, and run the cord down the central hole and out to one side. The bottoms of the four feet should be covered with felt.

For the benefit of those who have done some Venetian iron work or forging, we append Fig. 6, showing how a standard may be made by suitably bending four strips of metal and fitting them around a central brass tube, to the upper end of which the socket is attached, as shown in Fig. 7. The cord runs down this tube and then out to one side through a groove in the base.

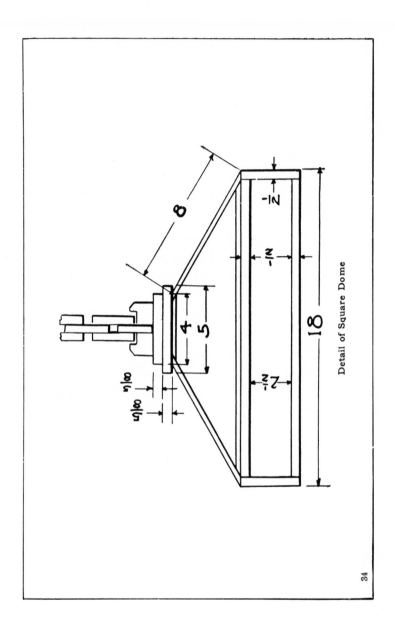

Detail of Square Dome

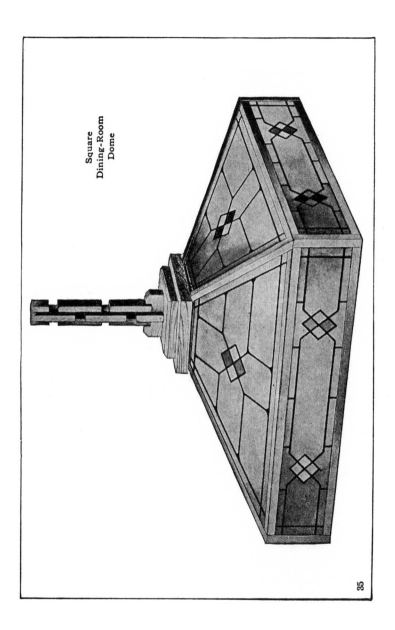

Square
Dining-Room
Dome

# CHAPTER IV

## SQUARE DINING-ROOM DOME

IN selecting the glass for a dining-room dome every consideration should be given to the general color scheme of the room. With any of the better forms of art glass, such as the mottled effects in green, amber or pink, no further decorative features need be added, beyond that afforded by the metal framing. It may be that nothing but the ordinary rough frosted glass is available, in which case a few added lines, suggestive of leaded glass, will not be inappropriate.

Of the various angle strips composing the frame, only the four lower ones and the short corner vertical members are exact right angles. If the reader has access to a machinery supply house, it would be well to procure a sufficient length of thin square brass tubing and form the angle pieces therefrom by filing off two diametrically opposite corners. In this manner perfect angles will be obtained which will form a very accurate foundation upon which the remainder of the structure may be built.

In constructing this piece some small clamps, or even spring clothespins, will be found convenient. Arrange the bottom angles squarely on the bench, or any convenient surface that is perfectly flat, and set in a few wire brads to keep them from shifting. Trim up the four vertical corner angles to the exact length and perfectly square on their ends. Set these in position with

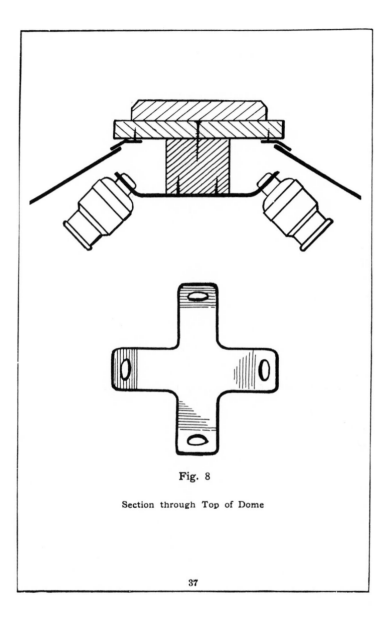

Fig. 8

Section through Top of Dome

clamps, and then attach their lower ends to the horizontal angles with solder. From the drawing determine the angle of the four angle strips that connect the top to the side panels, and, after the method illustrated in Fig. 1 (page 16), proceed to bend them from strips of brass about a fortieth of an inch thick. Cut these to length and trim their ends to the proper angle, after which they may be set up and clamped in place ready for soldering. The larger square block at the top is now to be made ready, and, after bending the four small top angle pieces, secure them to this block with small woodscrews. The block is now to be supported above the bench in its proper position relative to the framework thus far made, in which position the four slanting ridge angles may be fitted in place. When everything is correctly adjusted, proceed with the final soldering. Often a small alcohol lamp and blowpipe will be found much more convenient than a sol-dering-iron, as there is then no danger of disturbing the work. After soldering in some small clips to hold the glass (Fig. 3, page 23), the frame should be trimmed up with the file where necessary, any extra solder removed, and the whole rubbed bright with old emery cloth. The small top block is now to be made ready and applied, after which the electric fixture, for two, three or four lights as desired, must be placed. In Fig. 8 is a sectional view through the top of the dome, showing a four-light cluster improvised from ordinary sockets. A piece of brass about a sixteenth of an inch thick, in the form of a cross, has a large hole near each end, through which the nipple in the end of the socket may pass. By screwing the nipples up tightly the sockets are all held firmly in place, and may be arranged at the proper angle by bending the ends of the brass cross upward. A small block serves to maintain the lights at the proper distance from the roof of the dome.

The supporting chain may be of metal or wood. If of the latter material, the reader will find an easy way of constructing it described in Popular Mechanics handbook on "Arts-Crafts Lamps." The wires are run out through a hole in the top and follow up the chain to the ceiling.

# CHAPTER V

IN the construction of the four lanterns of this Mission chandelier a dull black finish in connection with plain frosted glass would be quite appropriate. The cost of the material will be insignificant if this arrangement is decided on, as all the metal frames may be of heavy tin painted a dull black.

Procure the four pieces to form the tops and a supply of 1-in. strips for the corner and bottom angles. Cut the top pieces to the pattern shown in the accompanying working drawing, and bend it along the dotted lines. Make the connection between the first and last sections with a few small rivets. Shape up the supporting loops from some heavy copper wire, flattening the ends so that they may be riveted to the top. Mark the positions of the corner angles and drill small holes for the rivets. The forming of the angles may now be undertaken as heretofore set forth in Fig. 1, that is, between wooden strips. In determining the proper lengths, allow about a half inch for bending over and riveting to the top, which operation may be attended to as soon as the angle strips are ready. The bottom angles are next to be gotten out and soldered in place, due care being taken that the frame is perfectly true and square. Into the inside angle of each corner piece solder a pair of small tin clips, to be bent over later to hold the glass. See Fig. 3, page 23.

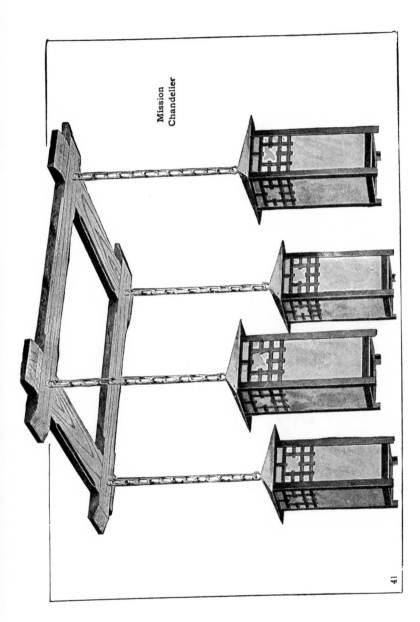

Mission
Chandelier

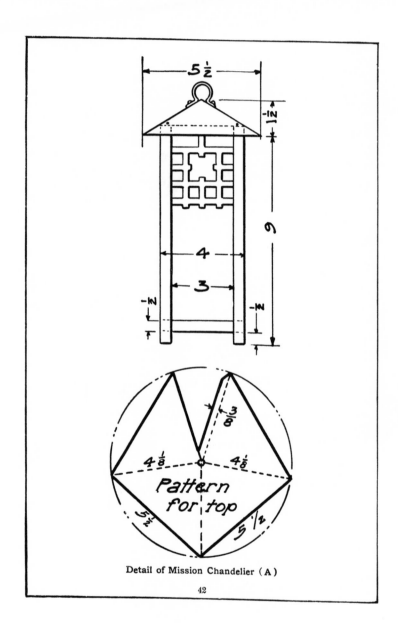

Detail of Mission Chandelier (A)

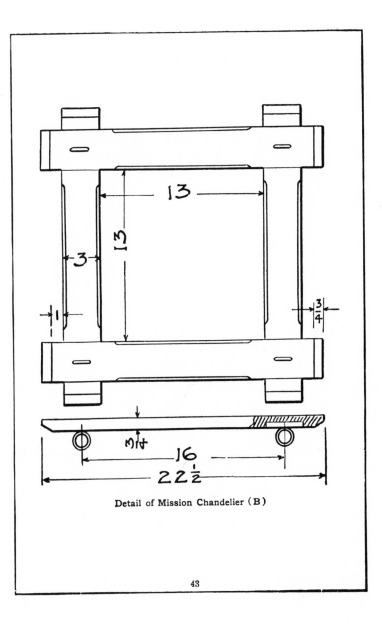

Detail of Mission Chandelier (B)

We now come to the lattice work, and here several methods present themselves. Sixteen in all are required. A very neat way is to get the necessary material in brass or copper and saw them out all at once with a small fretsaw. Another method is to etch them out with nitric acid. With very thin tin and a hardwood or lead block, they may be cut one at a time with a sharp knife. And lastly they may be cut, several at a time, from heavy black paper, and cemented to the glass panes.

All the metal should be thoroughly washed with soap and water, and dried, so as to remove any trace of the soldering fluid. Paint with drop black, and while this is drying proceed with the ceiling plate. This may be in the form of a cross, from each arm of which a lamp is suspended, or in the rectangular form shown. The four pieces are first to be trimmed up to the exact length, and then beveled off on their ends as shown. The joints are all crosslapped, that is, each piece of wood is reduced to one-half its thickness at the point of crossing, so that the two will fit together perfectly flush. Mark these connections out with pencil and square, and with all possible accuracy. Saw carefully and not too deep, after which the intervening wood should be slowly removed with a sharp chisel. The cutting and fitting completed, apply fresh carpenter's glue, and clamp until dry, taking due care that the assembled frame lies perfectly flat. When set, the edges are to be beveled off, and grooves cut in the upper side for the wiring. Sandpaper and apply the necessary stain. When dry, sand again, and if the wood is of an open texture, such as oak, apply a filler, thoroughly wiping off the surplus. This having dried, sand lightly and finish with a vigorous application of wax. It now only remains to set in four screweyes, connect the chains and lamps, and our chandelier is ready for hanging.

Desk Lamp with Soldered Shade

# PART TWO — SOLDERED SHADES

## CHAPTER I

### DESK LIGHT

IN this chapter the reader is introduced to an entirely different method of constructing lamp shades. This method, briefly stated, consists in binding all the edges of each piece of glass with thin metal, so that the several sections can then be soldered together. In this manner shades of almost any form may be built up, and in a truly substantial manner.

Let us accept as our initial problem with this mode of construction the making of the plain desk lamp illustrated. First procure the four pieces of art glass and some strips of thin tin about seven-eighths of an inch wide. These strips must now be bent into deep, narrow channels to fit over the edge of the glass. A very simple jig for accomplishing this is shown in Fig. 9. A strip of triangular section is nailed to a board, say about a foot in length. Adjoining this are two parallel strips, firmly secured to the board, but with narrow spaces between. Insert the strip of tin in the first narrow slit, as at A. Bend over with the edge of a piece of board to position B. Place the tin as at C, and then with a narrow strip of hardwood or iron force it clear down, so that when it is taken out

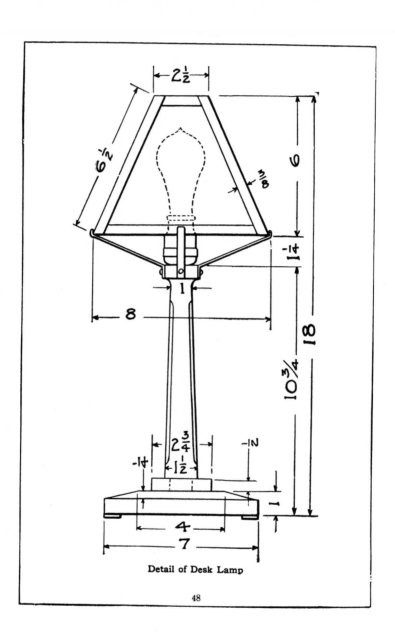

**Detail of Desk Lamp**

it will have the shape indicated at D. This latter slot should be slightly adjustable, so as to suit the thickness of glass. Be sure that between positions A and B the bending goes on uniformly along the entire length of the strip.

Having formed the necessary channels, proceed to fit

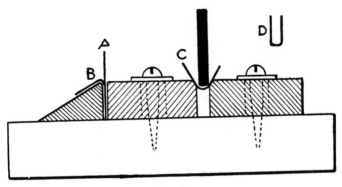

Fig. 9

Simple Jig for Bending Strips

them around the edge of the glass, cutting off any surplus with the file, as the tin-snips will crush the piece out of shape. When all four panes have been thus bound all the way round, heat the soldering-iron and fasten the overlapping pieces of tin at the corners. The four sections are now to be set up in their proper relative positions and held there while the soldering-iron connects the four corner seams. A cross section through a corner of the shade will be as in Fig. 10.

The tin is now to be washed and gone over with drop

black, which dries to a dull finish. With the second and following attempts the reader may use thin brass and copper in place of the blackened tin, although the latter is never out of place in a Mission interior.

The base should be treated in the usual manner—trimmed up true and square, and carefully marked with

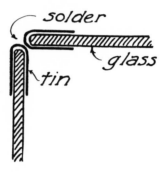

**Fig. 10**

Cross Section of Corner

guide lines prior to sawing off the beveled sections. Having worked the piece down to line, thoroughly sandpaper and then glue on the four small foot blocks. The half-inch block is now to be squared up and mortised in the center for an inch tenon. The standard will require some little care in working down to the proper taper and in forming the cap on top. After squaring up the piece of timber, mark out the guide lines (see Fig. 5, page 29) before cutting. Finish any two opposite sides down to line before starting a third. The socket is now to be fitted to the top, and a ⅜-in. hole drilled down the center for the electric cord, which passes out to one side underneath the base. The three pieces of wood are now to be glued together, and while the glue is setting, make ready the four small arms that support the shade. These may be of blackened iron, brass or copper. When the standard has been stained and waxed, attach these with screws, screw in the globe, place the shade, and turn on the current.

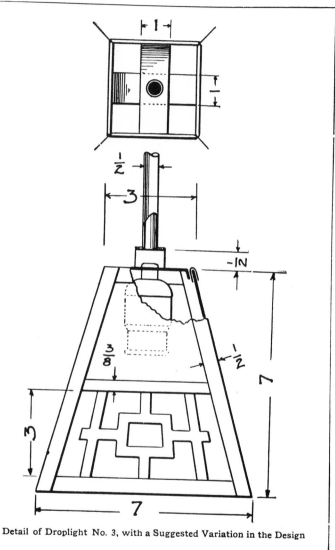

Detail of Droplight No. 3, with a Suggested Variation in the Design

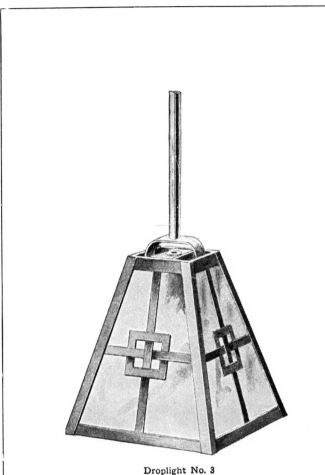

Droplight No. 3

# CHAPTER II

I N the initial chapter of this book are shown two forms of droplight shades having built-up frames. The accompanying illustration shows a third and somewhat larger form, and depicts a different mode of suspension. The reader will understand, of course, that many of these designs may be executed by some other method than the one that they are used to illustrate, and that such details as the suspending of the socket may be interchanged. The tapering shade, however, is particularly well adapted to the soldering method of construction introduced in the first chapter. In the one next following will be shown five of these shades used in connection with a chandelier.

The art glass should first be obtained, and a stock of thin metal strips—tin, brass or copper—laid in. The only practical way to get a good flat strip of tin without any twist is on the foot-actuated trimmer at the tinshop. A hundred strips may be cut in a few minutes with this device. The width of the strips will ordinarily be from ¾ in. to 1 in., depending somewhat on the size of the shade and the thickness of the glass. Always bend between wood, using some such jig as that illustrated in Fig. 9, page 49. In order to have the bend occur in the exact center of the strips, make a preliminary trial channel from a short piece about an inch or two in length. It will almost always be found best to place the top and bottom channels on each piece of glass before placing the side channels. The former should never come quite to the edge, whereas the latter should be full length. The horizontal and vertical crossbars are straight, flat strips

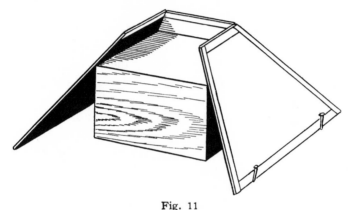

Fig. 11

**Holding the Panels in Position**

of metal, cut to such a length that their ends will fit a trifle under the edges of the border strips. In performing this operation take care not to bend the bars so much as to put a permanent kink in them, as they would not then lie flat against the glass. Before placing these they are interlaced through a hollow square—generally of the same metal, although copper is used in connection with brass with pleasing contrast. Having soldered the metal bindings at the four corners, and also tacked the crossbars, the assembling should be commenced. A good method of holding the four panels in position for soldering is shown in Fig. 11. The box in the center should be adjusted in height to the correct position and then tacked down. Accurately space off eight nails around so that the bottom edges of the panels will not slip outward. The illustration shows only three of the four glass panes in position.

The socket is supported by a plain piece of brass soldered across the top as shown in the working drawing. To this strip the socket is held by means of the nipple, as previously set forth in Fig. 2, page 19. A second strip bridges across the top about a half inch above the first and at right angles to it, and to this latter strip a $\frac{1}{2}$-in. brass tube is soldered. This tube is the main support and conceals the wiring. It may, of course, be entirely omitted, and the shade hung directly on the socket. Its presence is simply a matter of appropriateness with the conditions under which it is to be used. It will be noted that a variation in this shade is suggested in the working drawing.

# CHAPTER III

## CHANDELIER

E LABORATE though this chandelier may at first glance appear, its making in reality involves no constructive features other than those presented in the two preceding chapters. The shades are identical with the one shown in the last working drawing.

If the interior is in the Mission style, or on the bungalow order, a very good combination, and one that is quite inexpensive, is plain frosted glass used in connection with tin painted a dull black. In this case the brass hanging-tubes will be replaced with wrought-iron chains, also painted black. The exchange of the tubes for chains may be made when the shades are worked up in brass, in which case the chains will, of course, be of brass also. With the better grades of art glass, the mottled pink and amber effects go well with the plain brass finish, and the green tones with copper or blackened tin. When brass or copper is used, the soldering should, if possible, be done from the inside, and then rather neatly.

The dimensions of the ceiling plate are all given in the working drawing. If desired, the rectangular form of plate described in Chapter V of Part One may be used, in which case four instead of five lights will be used. In the present form, however, only one cross-lapped joint is necessary, and the carpentry in general is much

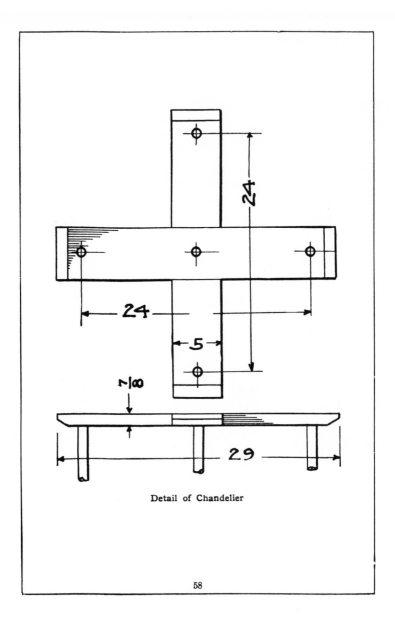

Detail of Chandelier

Chandelier with Soldered Shades

simpler. Each tube should be fitted clear through the wood and secured by a small plate or washer soldered on. Liberal grooves are to be cut along the upper face of the two members of the cross to receive the wiring, which may be tapped through the ceiling at any suitable point.

Even when the lights are to be controlled by a wall switch, it is often best to provide each shade with a drop pull, so that one or more of the shades may be darkened as desired.

# CHAPTER IV

## HEXAGONAL LIBRARY LAMP

FOR home construction there is but one practical method of making a large hexagonal shade, and that is the method, previously described, of binding all the edges of each piece of glass with thin metal and then soldering the bound sections together.

The six pieces of glass must be cut with all possible accuracy, because the final shape of the shade is entirely dependent on them. In Fig. 12 are given the dimensions of one section. As there are some rather sharp angles, fit four strips of paper around the glass, so that when they are flattened out again they will form correct patterns. Having procured the necessary number of strips of tin from the tinsmith, cut them up to agree with the paper patterns, accurately shaping the ends, so as to avoid subsequent filing. The strips are now to be bent into narrow channels that will closely fit over the edges of the glass. Fit on the top and bottom strips first. These pieces should not come quite to the edge of the glass. The side strips are then placed and soldered at their ends to the two strips previously placed. Any roughness or surplus solder should now be removed, and the six sections of glass set up ready for soldering together. A convenient method of holding them in place is illustrated in Fig. 11, page 55. The best soldering solution is that made by dissolving as much zinc as possible in muriatic

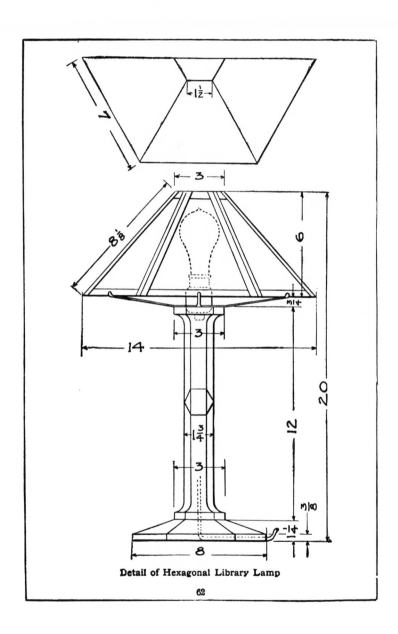

**Detail of Hexagonal Library Lamp**

Hexagonal Library Lamp

acid. The shade is now to be carefully washed with soap and water, and, when dry, painted with drop black, which dries with a dull finish.

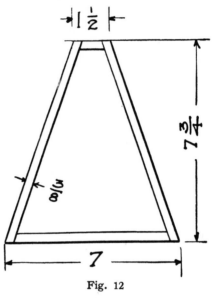

Fig. 12

Pattern Dimensions

In this lamp the woodwork will prove rather more exacting than usual, so that if the reader does not fancy this part of the task it might be well to substitute one of the standards previously described. The base block is first to be trimmed up to a true hexagon, after which carefully mark out all the necessary guide lines to aid in the sawing. The remainder of the task is simply one of patient application of the plane and sandpaper.

The standard should first be planed up to a hexagonal

section large enough to accommodate the 3-in. cap and base. The intervening column will then be worked down. In doing this choose the second face to be cut directly opposite the first. With two diametrically opposing faces smoothed down to line and parallel, additional guide lines may be drawn on them to facilitate the remainder of the cutting. The socket will next be fitted to the upper end, which should be hollowed out so as to let it set in for about three-eighths of an inch. Bore a hole down the center about the size of a lead pencil, so that the wires may be run down from the socket and out to one side through a groove in the base. Coat the lower end of the standard with glue to fill the pores, and when this is dry apply a second coat, after which the standard is to be attached to the base block with two or three screws set in from below. When dry, remove the surplus glue, sandpaper well and stain if desired. Filler should be applied to open-grained woods, such as oak. Finish with a thorough application of wax.

It now remains to provide three or six projecting arms to support the shade. These may be of brass strips screwed directly to the top of the standard, or soldered to a brass ring encircling the socket, which ring may then be fastened with screws to the top of the standard.

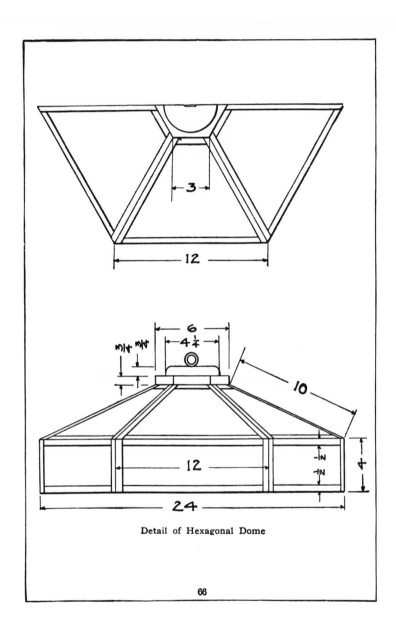

Detail of Hexagonal Dome

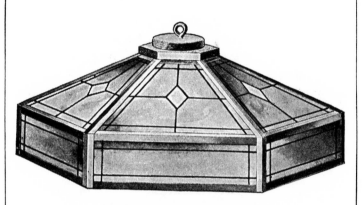

Hexagonal Dome for Library Lamp

# CHAPTER V

BEFORE proceeding to the third division of our subject we present herewith an attractive hexagonal dining-room dome—a lighting fixture which fully exemplifies
the possibilities of "soldered" shades. This method of
shade constructing has been fully described in the preceding chapters, and merely consists of binding all the edges
of each piece of glass with tin or other thin metal, which
is soldered at the corners. The various sections of glass
thus bound may then be soldered together.

Reference is again made to Fig. 9, page 49, which rep-
resents a jig designed to bend the thin metal strips into
channels without bends or kinks. Hammers, pincers and
the like will not produce uniform section, as the bending
must proceed uniformly along the entire length of the
strip at the same time.

The six vertical side sections are first to be bound and
soldered at their corners where the strips of tin overlap.
Set these up on some convenient and perfectly flat surface, bracing them by means of triangular blocks. This
method of bracing, but applied to a shade with only four
sides, is shown in Fig. 14. Test with the square, and then
solder the vertical seams. Fig. 13 gives the dimensions
for the slanting panels. Cut this shape out of cardboard,
and then apply it to the vertical sections to make sure that
it is correct, allowing, of course, for the metal binding to

be placed around the edges. When the glass for the six slanting sections has been cut, bind each section at the top and bottom first and then at the sides. Solder the overlapping corners of the tin strips and then remove any roughness. Next find some block or box to assist in the

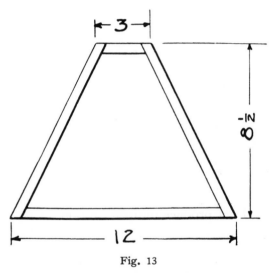

Fig. 13

Dimensions of Slanting Panels

setting up, and after adjusting it to the proper height, tack it down to keep it from shifting. The remaining sections may then be placed as in Fig. 14, and the four slanting corner seams soldered tight. With soap and water thoroughly remove all soldering acid, and then dry. Paint with a dull black paint. If brass or copper is used, simply tack the sections together at the top and bottom, after which the remainder of the seams may be soldered from the inside.

In Fig. 15 is shown the method of supporting the assembled shade.  A hexagonal block somewhat larger than the opening in the top of the shade is provided, and

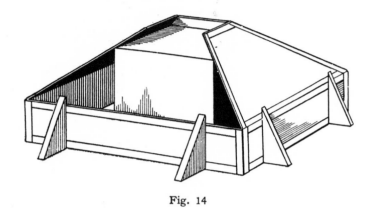

Fig. 14

**Method of Holding Sections in Position**

the shade placed upside down upon it, after which a thinner hexagonal block with beveled edges is dropped in and securely fastened down with screws.  A smaller block is finally placed on top, and a large screweye set in to connect with the chain.  In locating the point for this screw, make a preliminary test to be certain that the shade is perfectly balanced.

Fig. 15 also gives a very simple method of improvising a three-, four- or six-light cluster for the dome.  A piece of sheet metal about a sixteenth of an inch thick is cut

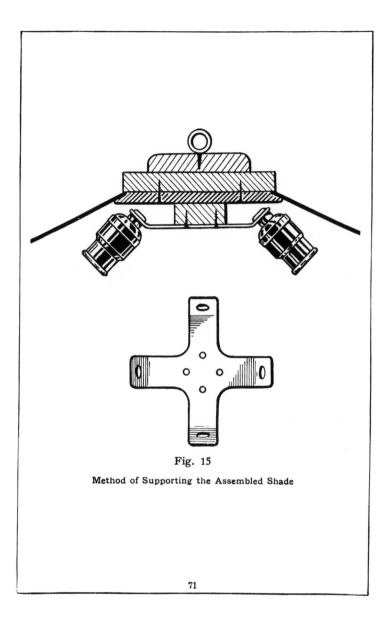

Fig. 15

Method of Supporting the Assembled Shade

with as many arms as there are lights. Drill a hole in each arm so that the nipple that screws into the top of the socket may be slipped through and set up tight. These nipples may be had for a few cents at any electrical supply store, and are usually two-ended, in which case one end must be removed with the hacksaw. In this manner ordinary sockets may be arranged in any form and at almost any desired angle by bending the ends of the projecting arms of the central piece. A square block attached in the roof of the dome affords a means of fastening the cluster in place. The wires are let out through a small hole in the top near the center and should then closely follow up the chain. A simple method of making a wooden chain is clearly set forth on page 26 of my book on "Arts-Crafts Lamps," in the Popular Mechanics Handbook Series.

Lamp No. 1 — Etched Brass

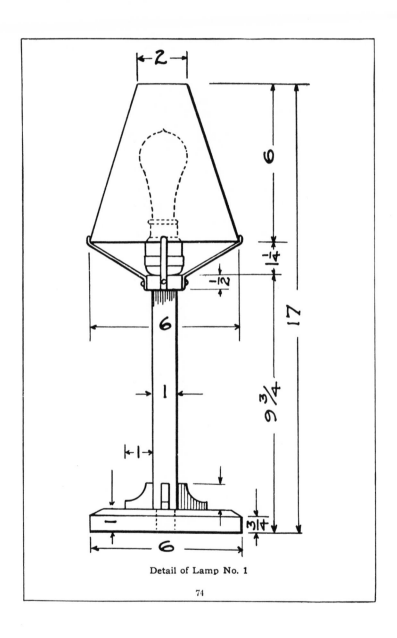

Detail of Lamp No. 1

# PART THREE — ETCHED SHADES

## CHAPTER I

### LAMP NUMBER ONE

ONE of the most interesting methods of making a lamp shade is that involving the process of etching. A piece of brass or copper is cut to the proper shape to form the shade, and is then painted with some acid-proof paint all over except those portions of the design that are to be eaten out. When dry, the metal is immersed in a solution of one part nitric acid to two parts water until the unpainted portions are eaten away. (*Caution:* Always pour the acid into the water, not the water into the acid. Pouring the water into the acid causes violent boiling and is extremely dangerous to hands and clothing). The sheet is then cleaned and bent in the form of the shade.

The advantages of this method are that designs of almost any degree of complexity may be worked out, and all without kinking or dinting the original surface of the metal. In fact, etching is the only method of handling real thin brass or copper for our purpose. This process will be set forth by drawings and descriptions of four portable lamps, which, for convenience, we will simply refer to by number, as the shade, the material for the lining, the base and standard, etc., are all subject to considerable variation.

In lamp No. 1 we make use of the square form of shade, having a cherry design etched through the metal, which should be about a fiftieth of an inch thick. Ac-

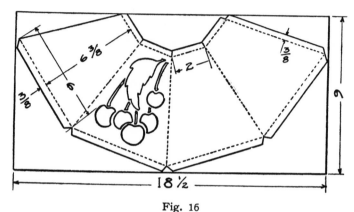

Fig. 16

Further Detail of Lamp No. 1

curately cut out the form of the side of the shade on paper, draw out the design, and then mark off the pattern four times on the metal, transferring the design by means of ordinary carbon transfer paper. Cut away the surplus metal with the tin-snips. Go over the lines with some sharp-pointed instrument, so that they will not be obliterated when the piece is washed and dried, which operation it must now undergo. Procure about ten cents' worth of black asphaltum paint or varnish, and paint the entire sheet of metal with the exception of the cherry design, which is to be eaten through.

If a large, flat tray for holding the etching solution is not at hand, one that will withstand the acid may be made of wood by lining it with pitch or tar. Melt the pitch in a can and pour it into the wooden tray, which

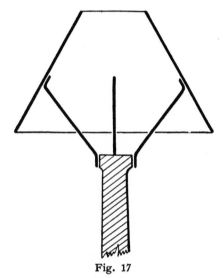

Fig. 17

Another Style of Shade Support

should then be tipped about in all directions until it is coated all over.

The etching solution is composed of one part nitric acid to two parts water. When the asphaltum is quite dry, immerse the piece, allowing it to remain until eaten through. Kerosene or turpentine will then be found convenient in removing the asphaltum, after which the piece is to be thoroughly washed and rubbed up bright with pumice or old emery cloth. The piece is now bent along the radial dotted lines in Fig. 16, which operation may be best done over the sharp edge of the table. The first and last sections are then connected by means of the extra strip provided for that purpose. The connection may be made by solder, small rivets or paper fasteners, as desired. The shade is now ready for the glass, which is held in place by bending over the extra strips at the top and bottom.

The base and standard of this little lamp are so simple as to require but little explanation. All corners must be kept sharp and square, and the lower end of the standard accurately mortised into the base block. Glue will be used on this connection and also to hold the four small bracket blocks in place. A three-eighths hole runs down the center to carry the cord from the socket. The four foot blocks are covered with felt attached with glue.

The supports for the shade may be of strips of brass or heavy copper wire flattened out on the ends so that they may be screwed to the upper end of the standard.

In Fig. 17 is suggested a second method of supporting a shade, in which the four supporting arms run well up into the shade and there engage some small clips provided for that purpose.

Lamp No. 2—Conical Form

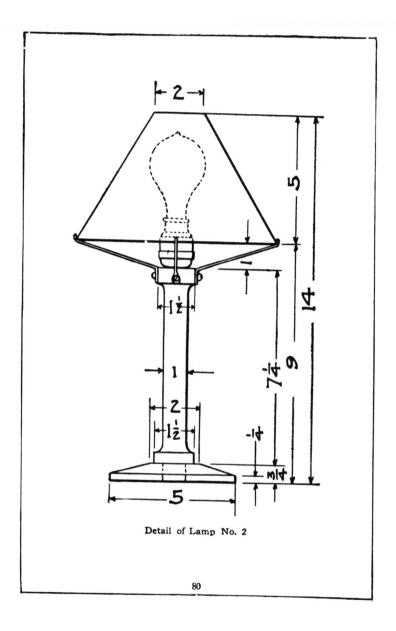

Detail of Lamp No. 2

# CHAPTER II

IN lamp No. 2 we make use of the conical form of shade and avoid the use of glass altogether, unless, of course, we happen to have on hand a suitable shade for which we wish to provide a brass or copper covering. The present design contemplates the use of colored paper, or some appropriate fabric, such as silk, for the lining of the etched metal frame. This fact, together with the gentle process of etching, which avoids practically all hammering, soldering and riveting, renders this process of lamp-shade construction especially adapted to amateur handicrafters of the gentler sex.

The process of laying out and etching will all be carried out as in the preceding article. Fig. 19 gives the necessary dimensions for drawing the pattern, but as the reader may desire a shade of different angle and diameter, a brief explanation will be given of the method of developing conical shades in general—a form of shade for which the etching process is particularly well suited.

Fig. 18 is a diagram intended to make this clear. Imagine the sides of the shade continued up to a point. If the cone thus formed is now rolled on a flat surface it will travel within a circle having a radius R, this radius being equal to the length of the slanting side of the cone. In the same manner the peak added to the shade, to complete the cone, will travel in a circle of radius $r$. There-

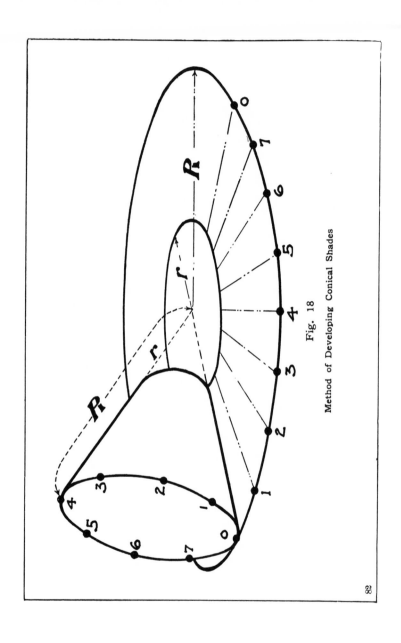

Fig. 18

Method of Developing Conical Shades

fore the desired pattern will lie between the two circles
of radii R and *r*. If the base of the shade is divided, for
example, into eight parts, then the points 1, 2, 3, etc. on
the shade will occupy positions 1, 2, 3, etc., on the circle
R. It will therefore only be necessary to measure off

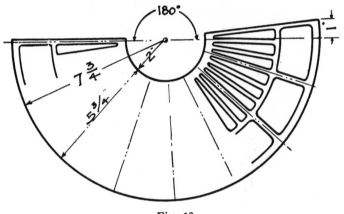

Fig. 19

Dimensions for Pattern of Lamp No. 2, with Suggested Variation in the Design

along the circle R a distance equal to the larger circum-
ference of the shade. In this manner a shade of any
angle or diameter may be drawn.

In rolling or bending an open-work shade, such as the
one illustrated, some little care must be exercised to obtain the true conical form. The very rigid pattern shown
was chosen for its simplicity, but any conventional flower
or fruit design may be worked out in the same manner.

If the metal is brass, it may be oxidized or simply
rubbed up bright, but in either case a coat of lacquer

should be applied to preserve the effect. Copper may be given an old effect by simply heating to the proper degree, and finished with lacquer or an application of wax and turpentine in equal parts. With the latter metal, a lining of sheer or raw silk of a rich green tone is particularly effective.

The most exacting feature in the construction of the wooden standard is the forming of the top and bottom projections. The piece of wood must first be squared up and marked with guide lines, as in Fig. 5, page 29, after which any two sides directly opposite may be worked down to line. These sides are then marked and the two remaining sides cut down, after which the hole through the center for the cord is to be bored. When the base has been beveled off and accurately finished, cut a mortise in the center for the standard and set up the joint with glue. After staining and waxing, screw on the four pieces of heavy copper wire to support the shade, which may then be placed.

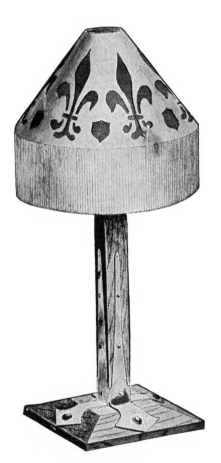

Lamp No. 3 — An Effect in Copper

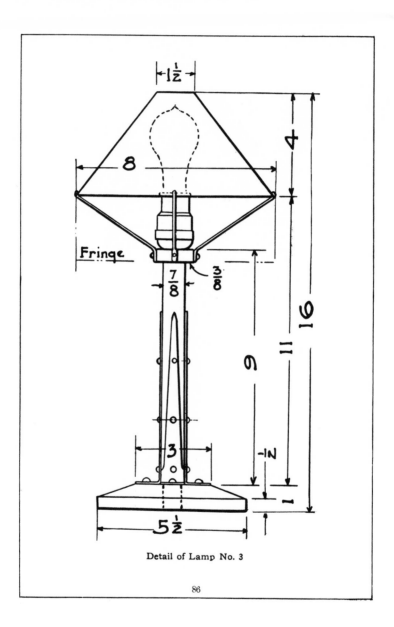

Detail of Lamp No. 3

# CHAPTER III

I N shades such as that on the lamp shown in the accompanying illustration, where the space occupied by the design is small in comparison with the total surface, some very artistic effects may be had by using copper, which colors so beautifully. The "waxed" finish has a soft satin sheen and is easily accomplished. The copper may be colored by heating or by an application of potassium sulphide and water, after which the highlights are rubbed up bright. Melt some beeswax and add an equal amount of turpentine. Heat the metal over a clean flame to such an extent that the wax will run. When cool, the surface is vigorously polished with a soft cloth. If the shade is of brass it may be colored by a solution of butter of antimony.

With lamp No. 3 we introduce the reader to the bead fringe, which may be purchased by the yard at a very reasonable price and in several colors. The lining of the shade may be of colored paper or silk, the effect of which can only be judged at night by holding it before a light.

Fig. 20 gives the dimensions necessary for the shade pattern, which, it will be noted, is divided into six parts. The number of these divisions will, of course, depend on the design chosen, but the dividing must be accurately done, else the irregularity will prove quite noticeable.

Such motifs as the grape and butterfly work up very well, and, when backed by the proper colors and illuminated, they are very pleasing indeed.

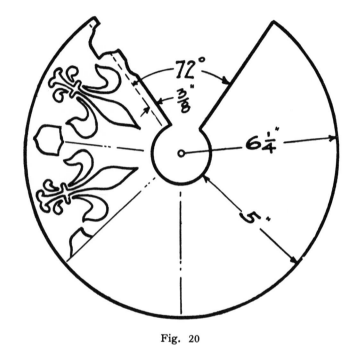

Fig. 20

Pattern Dimensions of Lamp No. 3

Having drawn out the large circles on the sheet brass, draw out the design on paper, and then transfer it to the metal, as many times as required, by means of carbon paper. Make the lines permanent by scratching with a sharp-pointed instrument, and then wash with soap and

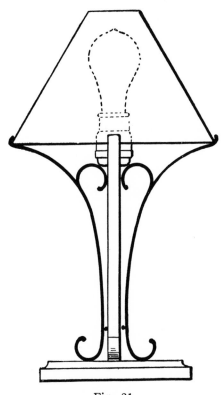

Fig. 21

Metal Standard for Lamp No. 3

water, prior to painting with the asphaltum varnish,
which is applied to all parts except the design.  When
thoroughly dry, immerse in the two-to-one nitric acid
solution, and allow to remain until etched clear through.
Remove the varnish with kerosene, wash again, and
polish with pumice or old emery cloth.  Carefully bend
into the conical form, fasten the ends with soft solder,
small rivets or paper fasteners, as desired, and proceed
to color as heretofore directed.  The shade is now ready
for the lining.

The base and standard of this lamp are rather attractive, considering their simplicity.  The base will first be
beveled off in the usual fashion and mortised for the
standard, which is then to be tenoned to match.  Drill
the central hole for the wires, and arrange the upper
end for the socket as previously illustrated in Fig. 4, page
24.  Set up with glue and test for squareness.  Stain as
desired, and when it is dry apply filler if the wood is
open-grained.  Finish with a good wax rub.  Get out
some strips of the same metal as the shade, and shape
them up into the four slender brackets.  These are then
finished like the shade and are attached with round-head
screws, or else large-headed upholstering nails.  Draw the
cord through, screw the socket in place, make and attach the four small arms that support the shade, which is
next to be applied, and our lamp is complete.

Fig. 21 will serve as a suggestion for a metal in place
of a wood standard.  The curved strips should not be
less than ½ in. wide, and, if of brass or copper, may be

readily bent as shown. The wires run up a central tube to which the socket is attached as shown in Fig. 7, page 32. If desired, the base may be of hammered brass or copper.

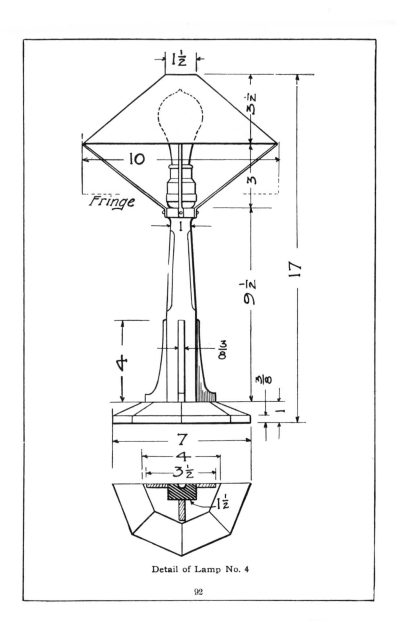

Detail of Lamp No. 4

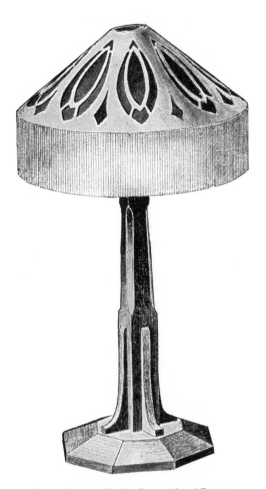

Lamp No. 4 — Simple Conventional Pattern

# CHAPTER IV

BEFORE taking up the lamp that is the subject of the accompanying illustration and the last one to be described having an etched shade, let us sum up the principal points of this method of shade-making. In the first place it should be remembered that art glass can only be used to advantage with the square and hexagonal forms. Colored paper and silk fabrics may be utilized in place of glass in a very attractive manner with the conical form of shade. Soldering, riveting and hammering are all unnecessary. The very thin metal used makes for lightness. The process of etching permits of designs of almost any degree of complexity to be worked out. The surface of the metal is always smooth and free from dints.

The present design makes use of a very simple conventional pattern on the shade. In these later days of so much stenciling the reader will not lack for suggestions along this line, and if complete and conspicuous harmony is desired in a room the same motif that is used on the walls and draperies may be worked into the shade.

Fig. 22 gives all necessary dimensions. The larger circles and the radial lines of the eight divisions may all be drawn directly on the metal, after which the design is to be drawn out full size on paper, from which it may

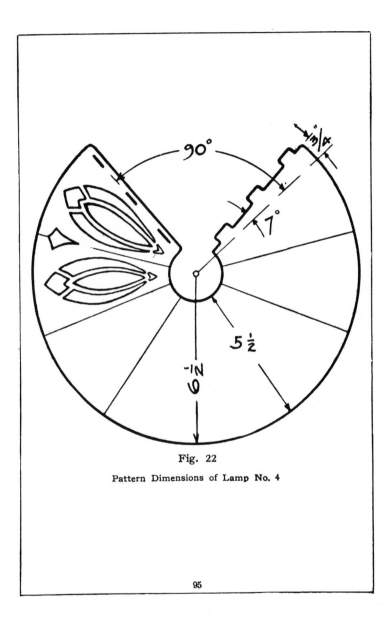

Fig. 22

Pattern Dimensions of Lamp No. 4

then be transferred to the metal eight times by means of carbon paper. Remove the surplus material from the edges and form the three projecting lugs, which will be used later in joining the two ends of the shade. The metal is now to be painted with asphaltum at all points except those that are to be etched clear through. Wax from an ordinary candle may be sometimes used to advantage on small pieces, which are heated so that the wax will run. The places to be etched are then scraped clean.

When the asphaltum has dried, immerse in the two-to-one nitric acid solution. A moderate bubbling after a few minutes indicates that the solution is of the proper strength. The fumes should not be inhaled, nor the acid allowed to touch the clothing or person. The etching completed, remove the paint with kerosene or turpentine, wash, dry, and polish with old emery. The metal is now ready for coloring and finishing by any of the methods previously described. The simplest finish of all is a plain emery rub, followed by lacquer.

The three slits into which the lugs, shown in Fig. 22, fit are now to be cut. Slowly and uniformly bend the shade into conical form, insert the three lugs into their respective slits and bend them over. The shade is now ready for the silk or paper lining and the bead fringe. Any small holes that may be necessary should be pierced with a fine point used over a block of lead or hardwood.

The woodwork is a trifle more elaborate for this than for the preceding lamps, as the octagonal form of the base will necessitate all possible accuracy. If, however, a true eight-sided block is first made and all possible guide lines are first drawn on it, the sawing and subsequent plane work will be greatly facilitated. The standard is first to be planed up square and to full size. The taper and cap will then be formed, and finally the four edges will be beveled off. Particular care should be taken to have the lower end perfectly square so as to leave no seam around the base block. The central hole for the cord is now in order, and then the four small brackets should be fitted and the whole made secure with glue. The socket is yet to be fitted (see Fig. 4, page 24), and a groove is to be made across the bottom to permit the cord to pass out, after which the wood finishing may be attended to. Arrange for the bracket arms that support the shade, and when these are attached and the electric bulb screwed in, nothing remains but the placing of the shade.

**Sawn Shade of Conventional Design**

# PART FOUR—SAWN SHADES

## CHAPTER I

### CONVENTIONAL PATTERNS

WE have now come to the fourth and last division of our subject, viz.: lamps with sawn shades. It is appropriate that this type should come last, because its construction is possibly the most exacting of all, which fact, however, is more than compensated for by the special attractiveness of this form of shade.

There is no set rule for the thickness of the brass or copper, except that, other things being equal, the larger the shade and the more open the design, the stouter should be the metal. Be sure that the metal lies perfectly flat. Cut out the pattern shown in Fig. 22½ on a piece of flat paper. Mark off the outline on the metal and then transfer the design by means of carbon transfer paper. Accurately retrace the lines with a sharp-pointed instrument so that they will not be obliterated while handling. In order that the material may remain flat, try to have it cut to size on the foot trimmer, otherwise the surplus must be sawn off. The tin-snips will have very little use in this work. Drill a small hole with the breast drill in each piece that is to be sawn out, so that the saw blade may be inserted. Fasten an overhanging block to the bench and cut a V slot in the end, as in Fig. 23. Insert the saw blade through one of the holes, place the sheet of metal on this block with the saw handle below, and proceed to saw with a slow uniform stroke. Always have the saw teeth pointing toward the handle, so that

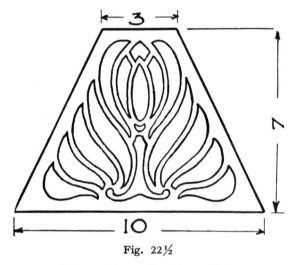

Fig. 22½

**Pattern of Conventional Sawn Shade**

the saw will cut on the pull stroke. Without a sawing-block such as this, very little will be accomplished. When all the pieces have been removed, the edges should be gone over with a small file, several shapes of which should be provided so that access may be had to all angles and corners.

In Fig. 24 are shown several methods of connecting the sawn sheets together at the corner angles. Method

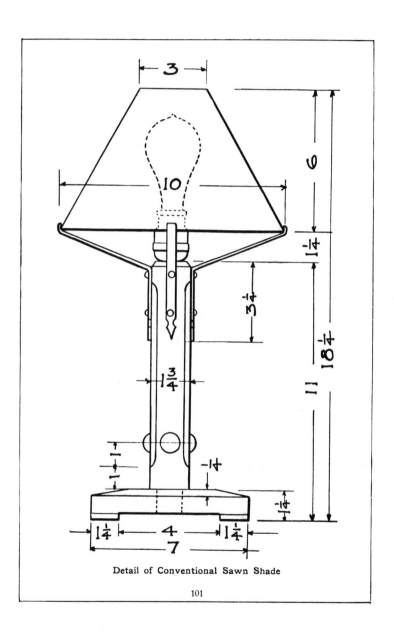

Detail of Conventional Sawn Shade

A is best used on heavy and accurate work and necessitates the use of solder, as does also method B.    Methods C and D are two of the easiest, as ample space is provided for riveting.

Having joined the sections, the four pieces of glass

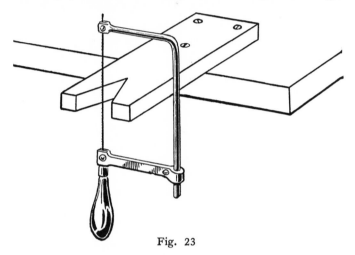

Fig. 23

Sawing-Block with V Slot

should be ordered and some small clips fastened inside to hold them securely in place.    Several ways of doing this are shown in Fig. 3, page 23.    Before placing the glass, however, the metal should be brightened, and oxidized if desired, and then coated with lacquer or finished with wax, as previously described.    For the conventional pattern illustrated the glass having a green effect is undoubtedly the most appropriate.

In the working drawing will be found all necessary dimensions for the woodwork, which is about as simple as possible. The socket should be of the pull-actuated variety and securely set into the top of the standard, through the center of which a ⅜-in. hole is to be drilled for the cord.

The four shade brackets are to be made rather heavy

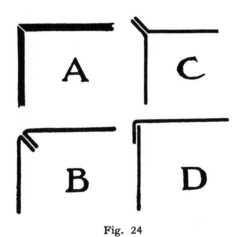

Fig. 24

Methods of Joining Sawn Sheets

—about ⅛ in. by ½ in.—neatly finished on their lower ends and drilled for wood-screws. If the ordinary round-head brass screws are used to attach these brackets to the standard, place each one in the breast drill and polish by rapidly rotating against a piece of old emery cloth. Before attaching these, the treatment of the wood should be attended to. If the surroundings will permit, a bog-green stain, followed by a coat of filler, well wiped off and sandpapered when dry, and then waxed, will be very appropriate.

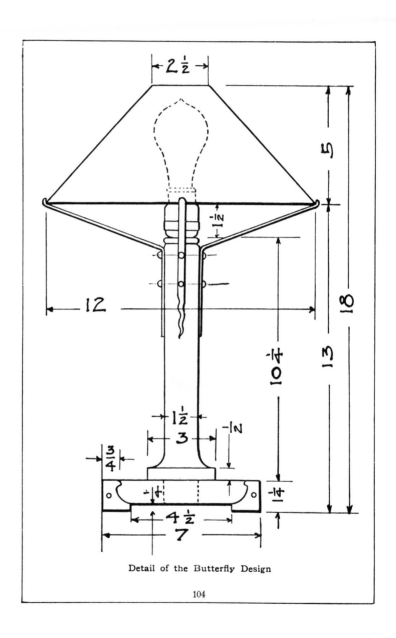

Detail of the Butterfly Design

The Butterfly Design

# CHAPTER II

## THE BUTTERFLY DESIGN

TO get the full effect of the accompanying design one should use art glass of an opalescent or pink shade, rather than any of the green or amber tones. There are also some decidedly iridescent varieties of glass that are very attractive with an oxidized copper finish. The butterfly design is a rather delicate one to saw, and may, if desired, be somewhat reduced and etched out to advantage on thinner metal.

Having decided whether the corner edges are to be bent out or in, soldered or riveted, as set forth in Fig. 24 of the previous article, the pattern should be drawn out in accordance with Fig. 25, and due allowance made for the corner joints. Any bending that is necessary should be done before soldering and while the plate is firmly clamped between stout hardwood strips, beyond which just the proper amount projects. The protruding strip may then be bent over with the edge of a straight piece of wood. Remember, however, that the angle may be considerably more or less than 90°, according to the nature of the corner connection and the angle of the sides. The sawing will proceed as heretofore directed, after which each of the four sheets should be closely inspected and gone over with a fine file to remove any imperfections and to work the pattern exactly down to line. Attach some small clips to the inner corners of the assembled shade, so that when the glass is inserted they may be bent over to retain it.

The base block is absolutely plain in this lamp and has four small blocks glued on the under side. Extending around each corner as far as these blocks are brass or

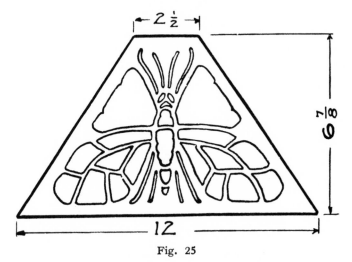

Fig. 25

Pattern Dimensions of the Butterfly Design

copper angles, fastened on with round-head screws or fancy upholstering nails. A square hole is mortised in the center to receive the tenon on the end of the stand-ard, which is now to be taken up. Dress the piece up full 3 in. square and trim off the ends squarely. Mark out the various lines to guide the saw, as previously shown in Fig. 5, page 29. After cutting down one side, proceed with the one directly opposite. When the two are worked down to line, guide lines may then be drawn on them to assist in cutting the other two sides. While the lines are all quite simple, the two pieces must be worked up with considerable accuracy and with good sharp corners; otherwise the effect will be entirely lost. The plainness of the top is relieved somewhat by cutting a small groove around it, after which the socket should be fitted in place. (See Fig. 4, page 24.) Before setting it, however, do not forget the central hole for the cord, which passes out under the base.

The four brackets that support the shade are now to be made ready, and in working out their lower ends to the sinuous point, see that the edges are kept sharp so as to fully bring out the shape. When these are drilled and attached, it only requires the placing of the bulb and the shade to complete the lamp.

The Pyramid Lamp

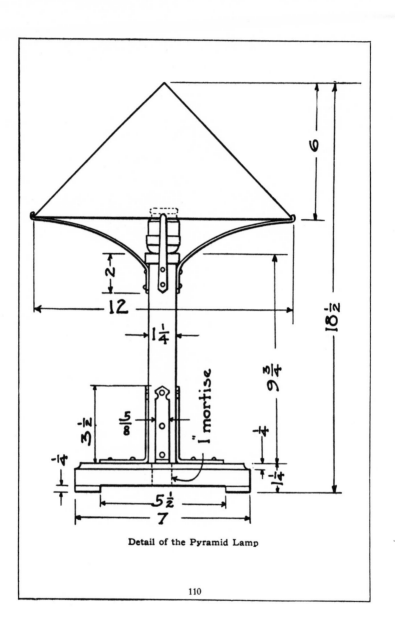

Detail of the Pyramid Lamp

# CHAPTER III

THERE are only two practical methods of making a pyramid shade—either etch it all from one large piece of metal and bend it into shape, or saw the four triangular sections from heavy brass or copper with such accuracy as to permit the forming of the sharp point. Let us confine ourselves to the latter method.

The four slanting corner connections will be made by beveling off the edges of the sheet metal with the file so that they may be soldered together as in Fig. 24 at A, page 103. After the sheets are all sawn they can be temporarily clamped in some improvised angle so as to hold them securely while soldering. Remember, however, that these angles are not right angles. While the soldering is in progress the clips to hold the glass in place should also be attached.

Fig. 26 gives the dimensions of the triangle; and as for the design, the reader has surely gone far enough in this series to devise something of his own, or at least adapt some other design in an attractive manner. Original work carries with it the true fascination.

The sawing completed, the edges of the pattern cleaned up with a small file, and the whole put together, the glass should be ordered, which is not to be left with any very sharp points, as a slight accident is apt to break them off and in so doing start a crack. Before inserting the

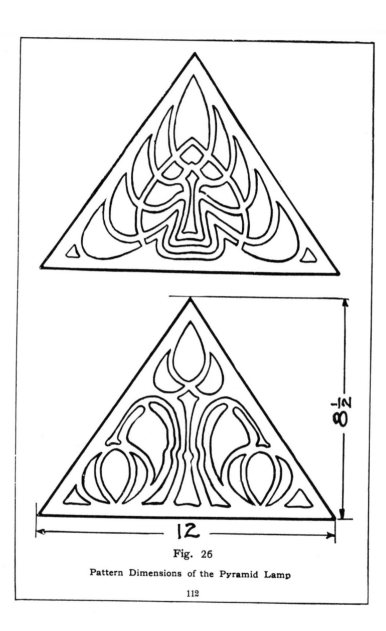

Fig. 26

Pattern Dimensions of the Pyramid Lamp

glass, brush up the shade with emery, and if an oxidized effect is not desired, the finish may be completed with a coat of lacquer. Brass can be oxidized with butter of

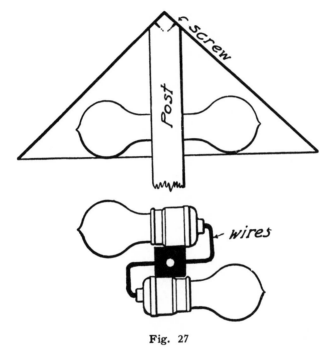

Fig. 27

Suggestion for Two Lights

antimony solution, and copper by one of potassium sulphide. Solutions may also be purchased for producing a verdigris effect that is particularly attractive on brass.

The base and standard are quite similar to several of those shown in the preceding chapters. Some little care will be necessary to get the end wood perfectly smooth and square, and also to form the quarter-round groove across the grain. Finish this groove with sandpaper wrapped on a round stick of the proper diameter. Mortise and tenon the standard and base together, and set up the joint with glue. Fit the socket to the top in the usual manner, and drill the central hole for the wires. Stain and finish the wood as desired, after which prepare the four metal brackets that support the shade and attach them with round-head brass screws. The bulb may now be screwed in, and the shade placed on and illuminated.

In Fig. 27 is a suggestion for providing such a lamp with two lights, and for supporting the shade without the use of the four bracket arms. The standard runs clear to the top of the shade, where it is pointed to the proper angle to fit the shade, which is then attached with small screws. If suitable fixtures are not at hand, solder a flat strip to the side of each socket, so that it may be fastened to the side of the standard. If the soldering is inconvenient, provide suitable strips bent so as to pass around the sockets and clamp them firmly to the standard.

# A CATALOG OF SELECTED
# DOVER BOOKS
## IN ALL FIELDS OF INTEREST

# A CATALOG OF SELECTED DOVER
# BOOKS IN ALL FIELDS OF INTEREST

CONCERNING THE SPIRITUAL IN ART, Wassily Kandinsky. Pioneering work by father of abstract art. Thoughts on color theory, nature of art. Analysis of earlier masters. 12 illustrations. 80pp. of text. 5⅜ × 8½. 23411-8 Pa. $3.95

ANIMALS: 1,419 Copyright-Free Illustrations of Mammals, Birds, Fish, Insects, etc., Jim Harter (ed.). Clear wood engravings present, in extremely lifelike poses, over 1,000 species of animals. One of the most extensive pictorial sourcebooks of its kind. Captions. Index. 284pp. 9 × 12. 23766-4 Pa. $12.95

CELTIC ART: The Methods of Construction, George Bain. Simple geometric techniques for making Celtic interlacements, spirals, Kells-type initials, animals, humans, etc. Over 500 illustrations. 160pp. 9 × 12. (USO) 22923-8 Pa. $9.95

AN ATLAS OF ANATOMY FOR ARTISTS, Fritz Schider. Most thorough reference work on art anatomy in the world. Hundreds of illustrations, including selections from works by Vesalius, Leonardo, Goya, Ingres, Michelangelo, others. 593 illustrations. 192pp. 7⅛ × 10¼. 20241-0 Pa. $9.95

CELTIC HAND STROKE-BY-STROKE (Irish Half-Uncial from "The Book of Kells"): An Arthur Baker Calligraphy Manual, Arthur Baker. Complete guide to creating each letter of the alphabet in distinctive Celtic manner. Covers hand position, strokes, pens, inks, paper, more. Illustrated. 48pp. 8¼ × 11.
24336-2 Pa. $3.95

EASY ORIGAMI, John Montroll. Charming collection of 32 projects (hat, cup, pelican, piano, swan, many more) specially designed for the novice origami hobbyist. Clearly illustrated easy-to-follow instructions insure that even beginning papercrafters will achieve successful results. 48pp. 8¼ × 11. 27298-2 Pa. $2.95

THE COMPLETE BOOK OF BIRDHOUSE CONSTRUCTION FOR WOOD-WORKERS, Scott D. Campbell. Detailed instructions, illustrations, tables. Also data on bird habitat and instinct patterns. Bibliography. 3 tables. 63 illustrations in 15 figures. 48pp. 5¼ × 8½. 24407-5 Pa. $1.95

BLOOMINGDALE'S ILLUSTRATED 1886 CATALOG: Fashions, Dry Goods and Housewares, Bloomingdale Brothers. Famed merchants' extremely rare catalog depicting about 1,700 products: clothing, housewares, firearms, dry goods, jewelry, more. Invaluable for dating, identifying vintage items. Also, copyright-free graphics for artists, designers. Co-published with Henry Ford Museum & Greenfield Village. 160pp. 8¼ × 11. 25780-0 Pa. $9.95

HISTORIC COSTUME IN PICTURES, Braun & Schneider. Over 1,450 costumed figures in clearly detailed engravings—from dawn of civilization to end of 19th century. Captions. Many folk costumes. 256pp. 8⅜ × 11¾. 23150-X Pa. $11.95

STICKLEY CRAFTSMAN FURNITURE CATALOGS, Gustav Stickley and L. & J. G. Stickley. Beautiful, functional furniture in two authentic catalogs from 1910. 594 illustrations, including 277 photos, show settles, rockers, armchairs, reclining chairs, bookcases, desks, tables. 183pp. 6½ × 9¼. 23838-5 Pa. $9.95

AMERICAN LOCOMOTIVES IN HISTORIC PHOTOGRAPHS: 1858 to 1949, Ron Ziel (ed.). A rare collection of 126 meticulously detailed official photographs, called "builder portraits," of American locomotives that majestically chronicle the rise of steam locomotive power in America. Introduction. Detailed captions. xi + 129pp. 9 × 12. 27393-8 Pa. $12.95

AMERICA'S LIGHTHOUSES: An Illustrated History, Francis Ross Holland, Jr. Delightfully written, profusely illustrated fact-filled survey of over 200 American lighthouses since 1716. History, anecdotes, technological advances, more. 240pp. 8 × 10¾. 25576-X Pa. $11.95

TOWARDS A NEW ARCHITECTURE, Le Corbusier. Pioneering manifesto by founder of "International School." Technical and aesthetic theories, views of industry, economics, relation of form to function, "mass-production split" and much more. Profusely illustrated. 320pp. 6⅛ × 9¼. (USO) 25023-7 Pa. $9.95

HOW THE OTHER HALF LIVES, Jacob Riis. Famous journalistic record, exposing poverty and degradation of New York slums around 1900, by major social reformer. 100 striking and influential photographs. 233pp. 10 × 7⅞. 22012-5 Pa $10.95

FRUIT KEY AND TWIG KEY TO TREES AND SHRUBS, William M. Harlow. One of the handiest and most widely used identification aids. Fruit key covers 120 deciduous and evergreen species; twig key 160 deciduous species. Easily used. Over 300 photographs. 126pp. 5⅜ × 8½. 20511-8 Pa. $3.95

COMMON BIRD SONGS, Dr. Donald J. Borror. Songs of 60 most common U.S. birds: robins, sparrows, cardinals, bluejays, finches, more—arranged in order of increasing complexity. Up to 9 variations of songs of each species. Cassette and manual 99911-4 $8.95

ORCHIDS AS HOUSE PLANTS, Rebecca Tyson Northen. Grow cattleyas and many other kinds of orchids—in a window, in a case, or under artificial light. 63 illustrations. 148pp. 5⅜ × 8½. 23261-1 Pa. $4.95

MONSTER MAZES, Dave Phillips. Masterful mazes at four levels of difficulty. Avoid deadly perils and evil creatures to find magical treasures. Solutions for all 32 exciting illustrated puzzles. 48pp. 8¼ × 11. 26005-4 Pa. $2.95

MOZART'S DON GIOVANNI (DOVER OPERA LIBRETTO SERIES), Wolfgang Amadeus Mozart. Introduced and translated by Ellen H. Bleiler. Standard Italian libretto, with complete English translation. Convenient and thoroughly portable—an ideal companion for reading along with a recording or the performance itself. Introduction. List of characters. Plot summary. 121pp. 5¼ × 8½. 24944-1 Pa. $2.95

TECHNICAL MANUAL AND DICTIONARY OF CLASSICAL BALLET, Gail Grant. Defines, explains, comments on steps, movements, poses and concepts. 15-page pictorial section. Basic book for student, viewer. 127pp. 5⅜ × 8½. 21843-0 Pa. $4.95

BRASS INSTRUMENTS: Their History and Development, Anthony Baines. Authoritative, updated survey of the evolution of trumpets, trombones, bugles, cornets, French horns, tubas and other brass wind instruments. Over 140 illustrations and 48 music examples. Corrected and updated by author. New preface. Bibliography. 320pp. 5⅜ × 8½. 27574-4 Pa. $9.95

HOLLYWOOD GLAMOR PORTRAITS, John Kobal (ed.). 145 photos from 1926–49. Harlow, Gable, Bogart, Bacall; 94 stars in all. Full background on photographers, technical aspects. 160pp. 8⅜ × 11¼. 23352-9 Pa. $11.95

MAX AND MORITZ, Wilhelm Busch. Great humor classic in both German and English. Also 10 other works: "Cat and Mouse," "Plisch and Plumm," etc. 216pp. 5⅜ × 8½. 20181-3 Pa. $5.95

THE RAVEN AND OTHER FAVORITE POEMS, Edgar Allan Poe. Over 40 of the author's most memorable poems: "The Bells," "Ulalume," "Israfel," "To Helen," "The Conqueror Worm," "Eldorado," "Annabel Lee," many more. Alphabetic lists of titles and first lines. 64pp. 5³⁄₁₆ × 8¼. 26685-0 Pa. $1.00

SEVEN SCIENCE FICTION NOVELS, H. G. Wells. The standard collection of the great novels. Complete, unabridged. First Men in the Moon, Island of Dr. Moreau, War of the Worlds, Food of the Gods, Invisible Man, Time Machine, In the Days of the Comet. Total of 1,015pp. 5⅜ × 8½. (USO) 20264-X Clothbd. $29.95

AMULETS AND SUPERSTITIONS, E. A. Wallis Budge. Comprehensive discourse on origin, powers of amulets in many ancient cultures: Arab, Persian, Babylonian, Assyrian, Egyptian, Gnostic, Hebrew, Phoenician, Syriac, etc. Covers cross, swastika, crucifix, seals, rings, stones, etc. 584pp. 5⅜ × 8½. 23573-4 Pa. $12.95

RUSSIAN STORIES/PYCCKNE PACCKA3bl: A Dual-Language Book, edited by Gleb Struve. Twelve tales by such masters as Chekhov, Tolstoy, Dostoevsky, Pushkin, others. Excellent word-for-word English translations on facing pages, plus teaching and study aids, Russian/English vocabulary, biographical/critical introductions, more. 416pp. 5⅜ × 8½. 26244-8 Pa. $8.95

PHILADELPHIA THEN AND NOW: 60 Sites Photographed in the Past and Present, Kenneth Finkel and Susan Oyama. Rare photographs of City Hall, Logan Square, Independence Hall, Betsy Ross House, other landmarks juxtaposed with contemporary views. Captures changing face of historic city. Introduction. Captions. 128pp. 8¼ × 11. 25790-8 Pa. $9.95

AIA ARCHITECTURAL GUIDE TO NASSAU AND SUFFOLK COUNTIES, LONG ISLAND, The American Institute of Architects, Long Island Chapter, and the Society for the Preservation of Long Island Antiquities. Comprehensive, well-researched and generously illustrated volume brings to life over three centuries of Long Island's great architectural heritage. More than 240 photographs with authoritative, extensively detailed captions. 176pp. 8¼ × 11. 26946-9 Pa. $14.95

NORTH AMERICAN INDIAN LIFE: Customs and Traditions of 23 Tribes, Elsie Clews Parsons (ed.). 27 fictionalized essays by noted anthropologists examine religion, customs, government, additional facets of life among the Winnebago, Crow, Zuni, Eskimo, other tribes. 480pp. 6⅛ × 9¼. 27377-6 Pa. $10.95

FRANK LLOYD WRIGHT'S HOLLYHOCK HOUSE, Donald Hoffmann. Lavishly illustrated, carefully documented study of one of Wright's most controversial residential designs. Over 120 photographs, floor plans, elevations, etc. Detailed perceptive text by noted Wright scholar. Index. 128pp. 9¼ × 10¾.
27133-1 Pa. $11.95

THE MALE AND FEMALE FIGURE IN MOTION: 60 Classic Photographic Sequences, Eadweard Muybridge. 60 true-action photographs of men and women walking, running, climbing, bending, turning, etc., reproduced from rare 19th-century masterpiece. vi + 121pp. 9 × 12.
24745-7 Pa. $10.95

1001 QUESTIONS ANSWERED ABOUT THE SEASHORE, N. J. Berrill and Jacquelyn Berrill. Queries answered about dolphins, sea snails, sponges, starfish, fishes, shore birds, many others. Covers appearance, breeding, growth, feeding, much more. 305pp. 5¼ × 8¼.
23366-9 Pa. $7.95

GUIDE TO OWL WATCHING IN NORTH AMERICA, Donald S. Heintzelman. Superb guide offers complete data and descriptions of 19 species: barn owl, screech owl, snowy owl, many more. Expert coverage of owl-watching equipment, conservation, migrations and invasions, etc. Guide to observing sites. 84 illustrations. xiii + 193pp. 5⅜ × 8½.
27344-X Pa. $8.95

MEDICINAL AND OTHER USES OF NORTH AMERICAN PLANTS: A Historical Survey with Special Reference to the Eastern Indian Tribes, Charlotte Erichsen-Brown. Chronological historical citations document 500 years of usage of plants, trees, shrubs native to eastern Canada, northeastern U.S. Also complete identifying information. 343 illustrations. 544pp. 6½ × 9¼.
25951-X Pa. $12.95

STORYBOOK MAZES, Dave Phillips. 23 stories and mazes on two-page spreads: Wizard of Oz, Treasure Island, Robin Hood, etc. Solutions. 64pp. 8¼ × 11.
23628-5 Pa. $2.95

NEGRO FOLK MUSIC, U.S.A., Harold Courlander. Noted folklorist's scholarly yet readable analysis of rich and varied musical tradition. Includes authentic versions of over 40 folk songs. Valuable bibliography and discography. xi + 324pp. 5⅜ × 8½.
27350-4 Pa. $7.95

MOVIE-STAR PORTRAITS OF THE FORTIES, John Kobal (ed.). 163 glamor, studio photos of 106 stars of the 1940s: Rita Hayworth, Ava Gardner, Marlon Brando, Clark Gable, many more. 176pp. 8⅜ × 11¼.
23546-7 Pa. $11.95

BENCHLEY LOST AND FOUND, Robert Benchley. Finest humor from early 30s, about pet peeves, child psychologists, post office and others. Mostly unavailable elsewhere. 73 illustrations by Peter Arno and others. 183pp. 5⅜ × 8½.
22410-4 Pa. $5.95

YEKL and THE IMPORTED BRIDEGROOM AND OTHER STORIES OF YIDDISH NEW YORK, Abraham Cahan. Film Hester Street based on Yekl (1896). Novel, other stories among first about Jewish immigrants on N.Y.'s East Side. 240pp. 5⅜ × 8½.
22427-9 Pa. $6.95

SELECTED POEMS, Walt Whitman. Generous sampling from *Leaves of Grass*. Twenty-four poems include "I Hear America Singing," "Song of the Open Road," "I Sing the Body Electric," "When Lilacs Last in the Dooryard Bloom'd," "O Captain! My Captain!"—all reprinted from an authoritative edition. Lists of titles and first lines. 128pp. 5³⁄₁₆ × 8¼.
26878-0 Pa. $1.00

THE BEST TALES OF HOFFMANN, E. T. A. Hoffmann. 10 of Hoffmann's most important stories: "Nutcracker and the King of Mice," "The Golden Flowerpot," etc. 458pp. 5⅜ × 8½. 21793-0 Pa. $8.95

FROM FETISH TO GOD IN ANCIENT EGYPT, E. A. Wallis Budge. Rich detailed survey of Egyptian conception of "God" and gods, magic, cult of animals, Osiris, more. Also, superb English translations of hymns and legends. 240 illustrations. 545pp. 5⅜ × 8½. 25803-3 Pa. $11.95

FRENCH STORIES/CONTES FRANÇAIS: A Dual-Language Book, Wallace Fowlie. Ten stories by French masters, Voltaire to Camus: "Micromegas" by Voltaire; "The Atheist's Mass" by Balzac; "Minuet" by de Maupassant; "The Guest" by Camus, six more. Excellent English translations on facing pages. Also French-English vocabulary list, exercises, more. 352pp. 5⅜ × 8½. 26443-2 Pa. $8.95

CHICAGO AT THE TURN OF THE CENTURY IN PHOTOGRAPHS: 122 Historic Views from the Collections of the Chicago Historical Society, Larry A. Viskochil. Rare large-format prints offer detailed views of City Hall, State Street, the Loop, Hull House, Union Station, many other landmarks, circa 1904–1913. Introduction. Captions. Maps. 144pp. 9⅜ × 12¼. 24656-6 Pa. $12.95

OLD BROOKLYN IN EARLY PHOTOGRAPHS, 1865–1929, William Lee Younger. Luna Park, Gravesend race track, construction of Grand Army Plaza, moving of Hotel Brighton, etc. 157 previously unpublished photographs. 165pp. 8⅞ × 11¾. 23587-4 Pa. $13.95

THE MYTHS OF THE NORTH AMERICAN INDIANS, Lewis Spence. Rich anthology of the myths and legends of the Algonquins, Iroquois, Pawnees and Sioux, prefaced by an extensive historical and ethnological commentary. 36 illustrations. 480pp. 5⅜ × 8½. 25967-6 Pa. $8.95

AN ENCYCLOPEDIA OF BATTLES: Accounts of Over 1,560 Battles from 1479 B.C. to the Present, David Eggenberger. Essential details of every major battle in recorded history from the first battle of Megiddo in 1479 B.C. to Grenada in 1984. List of Battle Maps. New Appendix covering the years 1967–1984. Index. 99 illustrations. 544pp. 6½ × 9¼. 24913-1 Pa. $14.95

SAILING ALONE AROUND THE WORLD, Captain Joshua Slocum. First man to sail around the world, alone, in small boat. One of great feats of seamanship told in delightful manner. 67 illustrations. 294pp. 5⅜ × 8½. 20326-3 Pa. $5.95

ANARCHISM AND OTHER ESSAYS, Emma Goldman. Powerful, penetrating, prophetic essays on direct action, role of minorities, prison reform, puritan hypocrisy, violence, etc. 271pp. 5⅜ × 8½. 22484-8 Pa. $5.95

MYTHS OF THE HINDUS AND BUDDHISTS, Ananda K. Coomaraswamy and Sister Nivedita. Great stories of the epics; deeds of Krishna, Shiva, taken from puranas, Vedas, folk tales; etc. 32 illustrations. 400pp. 5⅜ × 8½. 21759-0 Pa. $9.95

BEYOND PSYCHOLOGY, Otto Rank. Fear of death, desire of immortality, nature of sexuality, social organization, creativity, according to Rankian system. 291pp. 5⅜ × 8½. 20485-5 Pa. $8.95

A THEOLOGICO-POLITICAL TREATISE, Benedict Spinoza. Also contains unfinished Political Treatise. Great classic on religious liberty, theory of government on common consent. R. Elwes translation. Total of 421pp. 5⅜ × 8½. 20249-6 Pa. $8.95

MY BONDAGE AND MY FREEDOM, Frederick Douglass. Born a slave, Douglass became outspoken force in antislavery movement. The best of Douglass' autobiographies. Graphic description of slave life. 464pp. 5⅜ × 8½.    22457-0 Pa. $8.95

FOLLOWING THE EQUATOR: A Journey Around the World, Mark Twain. Fascinating humorous account of 1897 voyage to Hawaii, Australia, India, New Zealand, etc. Ironic, bemused reports on peoples, customs, climate, flora and fauna, politics, much more. 197 illustrations. 720pp. 5⅜ × 8½.    26113-1 Pa. $15.95

THE PEOPLE CALLED SHAKERS, Edward D. Andrews. Definitive study of Shakers: origins, beliefs, practices, dances, social organization, furniture and crafts, etc. 33 illustrations. 351pp. 5⅜ × 8½.    21081-2 Pa. $8.95

THE MYTHS OF GREECE AND ROME, H. A. Guerber. A classic of mythology, generously illustrated, long prized for its simple, graphic, accurate retelling of the principal myths of Greece and Rome, and for its commentary on their origins and significance. With 64 illustrations by Michelangelo, Raphael, Titian, Rubens, Canova, Bernini and others. 480pp. 5⅜ × 8½.    27584-1 Pa. $9.95

PSYCHOLOGY OF MUSIC, Carl E. Seashore. Classic work discusses music as a medium from psychological viewpoint. Clear treatment of physical acoustics, auditory apparatus, sound perception, development of musical skills, nature of musical feeling, host of other topics. 88 figures. 408pp. 5⅜ × 8½. 21851-1 Pa. $9.95

THE PHILOSOPHY OF HISTORY, Georg W. Hegel. Great classic of Western thought develops concept that history is not chance but rational process, the evolution of freedom. 457pp. 5⅜ × 8½.    20112-0 Pa. $9.95

THE BOOK OF TEA, Kakuzo Okakura. Minor classic of the Orient: entertaining, charming explanation, interpretation of traditional Japanese culture in terms of tea ceremony. 94pp. 5⅜ × 8½.    20070-1 Pa. $3.95

LIFE IN ANCIENT EGYPT, Adolf Erman. Fullest, most thorough, detailed older account with much not in more recent books, domestic life, religion, magic, medicine, commerce, much more. Many illustrations reproduce tomb paintings, carvings, hieroglyphs, etc. 597pp. 5⅜ × 8½.    22632-8 Pa. $10.95

SUNDIALS, Their Theory and Construction, Albert Waugh. Far and away the best, most thorough coverage of ideas, mathematics concerned, types, construction, adjusting anywhere. Simple, nontechnical treatment allows even children to build several of these dials. Over 100 illustrations. 230pp. 5⅜ × 8½.    22947-5 Pa. $7.95

DYNAMICS OF FLUIDS IN POROUS MEDIA, Jacob Bear. For advanced students of ground water hydrology, soil mechanics and physics, drainage and irrigation engineering, and more. 335 illustrations. Exercises, with answers. 784pp. 6⅛ × 9¼.    65675-6 Pa. $19.95

SONGS OF EXPERIENCE: Facsimile Reproduction with 26 Plates in Full Color, William Blake. 26 full-color plates from a rare 1826 edition. Includes "The Tyger," "London," "Holy Thursday," and other poems. Printed text of poems. 48pp. 5¼ × 7.    24636-1 Pa. $4.95

OLD-TIME VIGNETTES IN FULL COLOR, Carol Belanger Grafton (ed.). Over 390 charming, often sentimental illustrations, selected from archives of Victorian graphics—pretty women posing, children playing, food, flowers, kittens and ······ ··· ······ ·····-· ···d· ·nd butterflies, much more. All copyright-free. 27269-9 P· ·· ·

PERSPECTIVE FOR ARTISTS, Rex Vicat Cole. Depth, perspective of sky and sea, shadows, much more, not usually covered. 391 diagrams, 81 reproductions of drawings and paintings. 279pp. 5⅜ × 8½. 22487-2 Pa. $6.95

DRAWING THE LIVING FIGURE, Joseph Sheppard. Innovative approach to artistic anatomy focuses on specifics of surface anatomy, rather than muscles and bones. Over 170 drawings of live models in front, back and side views, and in widely varying poses. Accompanying diagrams. 177 illustrations. Introduction. Index. 144pp. 8⅜ × 11¼. 26723-7 Pa. $8.95

GOTHIC AND OLD ENGLISH ALPHABETS: 100 Complete Fonts, Dan X. Solo. Add power, elegance to posters, signs, other graphics with 100 stunning copyright-free alphabets: Blackstone, Dolbey, Germania, 97 more—including many lower-case, numerals, punctuation marks. 104pp. 8⅛ × 11. 24695-7 Pa. $8.95

HOW TO DO BEADWORK, Mary White. Fundamental book on craft from simple projects to five-bead chains and woven works. 106 illustrations. 142pp. 5⅜ × 8. 20697-1 Pa. $4.95

THE BOOK OF WOOD CARVING, Charles Marshall Sayers. Finest book for beginners discusses fundamentals and offers 34 designs. "Absolutely first rate . . . well thought out and well executed."—E. J. Tangerman. 118pp. 7¾ × 10⅝. 23654-4 Pa. $5.95

ILLUSTRATED CATALOG OF CIVIL WAR MILITARY GOODS: Union Army Weapons, Insignia, Uniform Accessories, and Other Equipment, Schuyler, Hartley, and Graham. Rare, profusely illustrated 1846 catalog includes Union Army uniform and dress regulations, arms and ammunition, coats, insignia, flags, swords, rifles, etc. 226 illustrations. 160pp. 9 × 12. 24939-5 Pa. $10.95

WOMEN'S FASHIONS OF THE EARLY 1900s: An Unabridged Republication of "New York Fashions, 1909," National Cloak & Suit Co. Rare catalog of mail-order fashions documents women's and children's clothing styles shortly after the turn of the century. Captions offer full descriptions, prices. Invaluable resource for fashion, costume historians. Approximately 725 illustrations. 128pp. 8⅜ × 11¼. 27276-1 Pa. $11.95

THE 1912 AND 1915 GUSTAV STICKLEY FURNITURE CATALOGS, Gustav Stickley. With over 200 detailed illustrations and descriptions, these two catalogs are essential reading and reference materials and identification guides for Stickley furniture. Captions cite materials, dimensions and prices. 112pp. 6½ × 9¼. 26676-1 Pa. $9.95

EARLY AMERICAN LOCOMOTIVES, John H. White, Jr. Finest locomotive engravings from early 19th century: historical (1804–74), main-line (after 1870), special, foreign, etc. 147 plates. 142pp. 11⅜ × 8¼. 22772-3 Pa. $10.95

THE TALL SHIPS OF TODAY IN PHOTOGRAPHS, Frank O. Braynard. Lavishly illustrated tribute to nearly 100 majestic contemporary sailing vessels: Amerigo Vespucci, Clearwater, Constitution, Eagle, Mayflower, Sea Cloud, Victory, many more. Authoritative captions provide statistics, background on each ship. 190 black-and-white photographs and illustrations. Introduction. 128pp. 8⅞ × 11¾. 27163-3 Pa. $13.95

EARLY NINETEENTH-CENTURY CRAFTS AND TRADES, Peter Stockham (ed.). Extremely rare 1807 volume describes to youngsters the crafts and trades of the day: brickmaker, weaver, dressmaker, bookbinder, ropemaker, saddler, many more. Quaint prose, charming illustrations for each craft. 20 black-and-white line illustrations. 192pp. 4⅝ × 6. 27293-1 Pa. $4.95

VICTORIAN FASHIONS AND COSTUMES FROM HARPER'S BAZAR, 1867–1898, Stella Blum (ed.). Day costumes, evening wear, sports clothes, shoes, hats, other accessories in over 1,000 detailed engravings. 320pp. 9⅜ × 12¼.
22990-4 Pa. $13.95

GUSTAV STICKLEY, THE CRAFTSMAN, Mary Ann Smith. Superb study surveys broad scope of Stickley's achievement, especially in architecture. Design philosophy, rise and fall of the Craftsman empire, descriptions and floor plans for many Craftsman houses, more. 86 black-and-white halftones. 31 line illustrations. Introduction. 208pp. 6½ × 9¼. 27210-9 Pa. $9.95

THE LONG ISLAND RAIL ROAD IN EARLY PHOTOGRAPHS, Ron Ziel. Over 220 rare photos, informative text document origin (1844) and development of rail service on Long Island. Vintage views of early trains, locomotives, stations, passengers, crews, much more. Captions. 8⅞ × 11¾. 26301-0 Pa. $13.95

THE BOOK OF OLD SHIPS: From Egyptian Galleys to Clipper Ships, Henry B. Culver. Superb, authoritative history of sailing vessels, with 80 magnificent line illustrations. Galley, bark, caravel, longship, whaler, many more. Detailed, informative text on each vessel by noted naval historian. Introduction. 256pp. 5⅜ × 8½. 27332-6 Pa. $6.95

TEN BOOKS ON ARCHITECTURE, Vitruvius. The most important book ever written on architecture. Early Roman aesthetics, technology, classical orders, site selection, all other aspects. Morgan translation. 331pp. 5⅜ × 8½. 20645-9 Pa. $8.95

THE HUMAN FIGURE IN MOTION, Eadweard Muybridge. More than 4,500 stopped-action photos, in action series, showing undraped men, women, children jumping, lying down, throwing, sitting, wrestling, carrying, etc. 390pp. 7⅞ × 10⅝.
20204-6 Clothbd. $24.95

TREES OF THE EASTERN AND CENTRAL UNITED STATES AND CANADA, William M. Harlow. Best one-volume guide to 140 trees. Full descriptions, woodlore, range, etc. Over 600 illustrations. Handy size. 288pp. 4½ × 6⅜.
20395-6 Pa. $5.95

SONGS OF WESTERN BIRDS, Dr. Donald J. Borror. Complete song and call repertoire of 60 western species, including flycatchers, juncoes, cactus wrens, many more—includes fully illustrated booklet. Cassette and manual 99913-0 $8.95

GROWING AND USING HERBS AND SPICES, Milo Miloradovich. Versatile handbook provides all the information needed for cultivation and use of all the herbs and spices available in North America. 4 illustrations. Index. Glossary. 236pp. 5⅜ × 8½. 25058-X Pa. $6.95

BIG BOOK OF MAZES AND LABYRINTHS, Walter Shepherd. 50 mazes and labyrinths in all—classical, solid, ripple, and more—in one great volume. Perfect inexpensive puzzler for clever youngsters. Full solutions. 112pp. 8⅛ × 11.
22951-3 Pa. $4.95

PIANO TUNING, J. Cree Fischer. Clearest, best book for beginner, amateur. Simple repairs, raising dropped notes, tuning by easy method of flattened fifths. No previous skills needed. 4 illustrations. 201pp. 5⅜ × 8½.                  23267-0 Pa. $5.95

A SOURCE BOOK IN THEATRICAL HISTORY, A. M. Nagler. Contemporary observers on acting, directing, make-up, costuming, stage props, machinery, scene design, from Ancient Greece to Chekhov. 611pp. 5⅜ × 8½.          20515-0 Pa. $11.95

THE COMPLETE NONSENSE OF EDWARD LEAR, Edward Lear. All nonsense limericks, zany alphabets, Owl and Pussycat, songs, nonsense botany, etc., illustrated by Lear. Total of 320pp. 5⅜ × 8½. (USO)              20167-8 Pa. $6.95

VICTORIAN PARLOUR POETRY: An Annotated Anthology, Michael R. Turner. 117 gems by Longfellow, Tennyson, Browning, many lesser-known poets. "The Village Blacksmith," "Curfew Must Not Ring Tonight," "Only a Baby Small," dozens more, often difficult to find elsewhere. Index of poets, titles, first lines. xxiii + 325pp. 5⅜ × 8¼.                  27044-0 Pa. $8.95

DUBLINERS, James Joyce. Fifteen stories offer vivid, tightly focused observations of the lives of Dublin's poorer classes. At least one, "The Dead," is considered a masterpiece. Reprinted complete and unabridged from standard edition. 160pp. 5³⁄₁₆ × 8¼.                  26870-5 Pa. $1.00

THE HAUNTED MONASTERY and THE CHINESE MAZE MURDERS, Robert van Gulik. Two full novels by van Gulik, set in 7th-century China, continue adventures of Judge Dee and his companions. An evil Taoist monastery, seemingly supernatural events; overgrown topiary maze hides strange crimes. 27 illustrations. 328pp. 5⅜ × 8½.                  23502-5 Pa. $7.95

THE BOOK OF THE SACRED MAGIC OF ABRAMELIN THE MAGE, translated by S. MacGregor Mathers. Medieval manuscript of ceremonial magic. Basic document in Aleister Crowley, Golden Dawn groups. 268pp. 5⅜ × 8½.
                  23211-5 Pa. $8.95

NEW RUSSIAN-ENGLISH AND ENGLISH-RUSSIAN DICTIONARY, M. A. O'Brien. This is a remarkably handy Russian dictionary, containing a surprising amount of information, including over 70,000 entries. 366pp. 4½ × 6⅛.
                  20208-9 Pa. $9.95

HISTORIC HOMES OF THE AMERICAN PRESIDENTS, Second, Revised Edition, Irvin Haas. A traveler's guide to American Presidential homes, most open to the public, depicting and describing homes occupied by every American President from George Washington to George Bush. With visiting hours, admission charges, travel routes. 175 photographs. Index. 160pp. 8¼ × 11. 26751-2 Pa. $10.95

NEW YORK IN THE FORTIES, Andreas Feininger. 162 brilliant photographs by the well-known photographer, formerly with *Life* magazine. Commuters, shoppers, Times Square at night, much else from city at its peak. Captions by John von Hartz. 181pp. 9¼ × 10¾.                  23585-8 Pa. $12.95

INDIAN SIGN LANGUAGE, William Tomkins. Over 525 signs developed by Sioux and other tribes. Written instructions and diagrams. Also 290 pictographs. 111pp. 6⅛ × 9¼.                  22029-

THE INFLUENCE OF SEA POWER UPON HISTORY, 1660–1783, A. T. Mahan. Influential classic of naval history and tactics still used as text in war colleges. First paperback edition. 4 maps. 24 battle plans. 640pp. 5⅜ × 8½.
25509-3 Pa. $12.95

THE STORY OF THE TITANIC AS TOLD BY ITS SURVIVORS, Jack Winocour (ed.). What it was really like. Panic, despair, shocking inefficiency, and a little heroism. More thrilling than any fictional account. 26 illustrations. 320pp. 5⅜ × 8½.
**20610-6 Pa. $8.95**

FAIRY AND FOLK TALES OF THE IRISH PEASANTRY, William Butler Yeats (ed.). Treasury of 64 tales from the twilight world of Celtic myth and legend: "The Soul Cages," "The Kildare Pooka," "King O'Toole and his Goose," many more. Introduction and Notes by W. B. Yeats. 352pp. 5⅜ × 8½. **26941-8 Pa. $8.95**

BUDDHIST MAHAYANA TEXTS, E. B. Cowell and Others (eds.). Superb, accurate translations of basic documents in Mahayana Buddhism, highly important in history of religions. The Buddha-karita of Asvaghosha, Larger Sukhavativyuha, more. 448pp. 5⅜ × 8½. 25552-2 Pa. $9.95

ONE TWO THREE . . . INFINITY: Facts and Speculations of Science, George Gamow. Great physicist's fascinating, readable overview of contemporary science: number theory, relativity, fourth dimension, entropy, genes, atomic structure, much more. 128 illustrations. Index. 352pp. 5⅜ × 8½. **25664-2 Pa. $8.95**

ENGINEERING IN HISTORY, Richard Shelton Kirby, et al. Broad, nontechnical survey of history's major technological advances: birth of Greek science, industrial revolution, electricity and applied science, 20th-century automation, much more. 181 illustrations. ". . . excellent . . ."—Isis. Bibliography. vii + 530pp. 5⅜ × 8¼.
26412-2 Pa. $14.95

*Prices subject to change without notice.*

Available at your book dealer or write for free catalog to Dept. GI, Dover Publications, Inc., 31 East 2nd St., Mineola, N.Y. 11501. Dover publishes more than 500 books each year on science, elementary and advanced mathematics, biology, music, art, literary history, social sciences and other areas.